Thinking Critically

Thinking Critically: Teen Suicide

Bradley Steffens

ReferencePoint
Press®

San Diego, CA

© 2019 ReferencePoint Press, Inc.
Printed in the United States

For more information, contact:
ReferencePoint Press, Inc.
PO Box 27779
San Diego, CA 92198
www.ReferencePointPress.com

Picture Credits:
All charts and graphs by Maury Aaseng.

LIBRARY OF CONGRESS CATALOGING-IN-PUBLICATION DATA

Name: Steffens, Bradley, 1955– author.
Title: Thinking Critically: Teen Suicide/by Bradley Steffens.
Description: San Diego, CA: ReferencePoint Press, Inc., [2019] | Series: Thinking Critically | Includes bibliographical references and index.
Identifiers: LCCN 2017053665 (print) | LCCN 2017056814 (ebook) | ISBN 9781682824481 (eBook) | ISBN 9781682824474 (hardback)
Subjects: LCSH: Teenagers—Suicidal behavior—United States—Juvenile literature. | Suicide—United States—Juvenile literature. | Suicide—Prevention—Juvenile literature.
Classification: LCC HV6546 (ebook) | LCC HV6546 .S74 2019 (print) | DDC 362.280835/0973—dc23
LC record available at https://lccn.loc.gov/2017053665

Contents

Foreword

"Literacy is the most basic currency of the knowledge economy we're living in today." Barack Obama (at the time a senator from Illinois) spoke these words during a 2005 speech before the American Library Association. One question raised by this statement is: What does it mean to be a literate person in the twenty-first century?

E.D. Hirsch Jr., author of *Cultural Literacy: What Every American Needs to Know*, answers the question this way: "To be culturally literate is to possess the basic information needed to thrive in the modern world. The breadth of the information is great, extending over the major domains of human activity from sports to science."

But literacy in the twenty-first century goes beyond the accumulation of knowledge gained through study and experience and expanded over time. Now more than ever literacy requires the ability to sift through and evaluate vast amounts of information and, as the authors of the Common Core State Standards state, to "demonstrate the cogent reasoning and use of evidence that is essential to both private deliberation and responsible citizenship in a democratic republic."

The *Thinking Critically* series challenges students to become discerning readers, to think independently, and to engage and develop their skills as critical thinkers. Through a narrative-driven, pro/con format, the series introduces students to the complex issues that dominate public discourse—topics such as gun control and violence, social networking, and medical marijuana. Each chapter revolves around a single, pointed question such as Can Stronger Gun Control Measures Prevent Mass Shootings?, or Does Social Networking Benefit Society?, or Should Medical Marijuana Be Legalized? This inquiry-based approach introduces student researchers to core issues and concerns on a given topic. Each chapter includes one part that argues the affirmative and one part that argues the negative—all written by a single author. With the single-author format the predominant arguments for and against an issue can be synthesized into clear, accessible discussions supported by details and evidence including relevant facts, direct quotes, current examples, and statistical illustrations. All volumes include focus questions to guide students as they read each pro/con discussion, a list of key facts, and an annotated list of related organizations and websites for conducting further research.

The authors of the Common Core State Standards have set out the particular qualities that a literate person in the twenty-first century must have. These include the ability to think independently, establish a base of knowledge across a wide range of subjects, engage in open-minded but discerning reading and listening, know how to use and evaluate evidence, and appreciate and understand diverse perspectives. The new *Thinking Critically* series supports these goals by providing a solid introduction to the study of pro/con issues.

A Deadly Epidemic

The news from the Centers for Disease Control and Prevention (CDC) was shocking: In 2016 suicide in the United States surged to its highest level in nearly thirty years. In 2016 (the most recent year of available death data), 44,876 deaths in the United States were the result of suicide. Between 2007 and 2017, the rate of suicide increased in nearly every age group, including teens. In that time frame, suicide became the second-leading cause of death of people age ten to twenty-four, behind only accidental death. "It's really stunning to see such a large increase in suicide rates affecting virtually every age group,"[1] says Katherine Hempstead, senior adviser for health care at the Robert Wood Johnson Foundation, a public health organization.

The phenomenon is not restricted to the United States. The World Health Organization (WHO) reports that more than eight hundred thousand people worldwide take their lives every year—more than the number who die from all homicides and wars combined. The death toll includes a rising number of teen suicides. "In the 1990s, I would have had one or two attempted suicides a year," says Julie Lynn Evans, a child psychotherapist in Somerset, England. "Now, I could have as many as four a month."[2]

A Surge Among Teenage Girls

The increase of suicide rates among teenage girls is especially alarming. The number of suicides among girls age ten to fourteen tripled between 1999 and 2014, while the number for boys in that age group grew by 43 percent. One of the reasons that the rate of increase is greater for girls than for boys is that fewer girls take their lives overall, so even a moderate increase in their numbers is expressed as a large percentage of growth. For example, in 2014 there were four times as many deaths among young men age fifteen to twenty-four as there were among young women in the same age group—4,089 compared to 990. This is in part because boys and men tend to use more lethal methods than girls and women do. According to the CDC, firearms are the most com-

> "In the 1990s, I would have had one or two attempted suicides a year. Now, I could have as many as four a month."[2]
>
> —Julie Lynn Evans, child psychotherapist

monly used method of suicide among males, while poisoning is the most common method of suicide for females. Chillingly, the CDC believes the numbers of teen suicides might actually be greater than the reports indicate. Officials suggest that some deaths from drug overdoses, traffic accidents, and firearm accidents might actually be suicides.

The Definition of Suicide

The fuzzy line between deadly accidents and suicide is reflected in the CDC's definition of suicide. The CDC places suicide as part of a broader class of behavior called self-directed violence. This term refers to any action a person takes toward oneself that deliberately results in injury or the potential for injury. Not all self-directed violence is suicidal. Some people cut themselves or harm themselves in other ways that are not intended to take their lives. Other self-directed violence is meant to result in death but does not. The CDC classifies such actions as suicide attempts. The CDC defines the terms this way:

> **Suicide** is a death caused by self-directed injurious behavior with any intent to die as a result of the behavior.
> **Suicide attempt** is defined as a non-fatal self-directed and potentially injurious behavior with any intent to die as a result of the behavior. A suicide attempt may or may not result in injury.[3]

According to the American Association of Suicidology, for every person who dies by suicide, more than thirty others attempt suicide and survive.

Teen Suicide Rates Are Rising

Suicide rates for US teens have been steadily rising since 2007, according to a 2017 report by the Centers for Disease Control and Prevention. The suicide rate for girls age fifteen to nineteen doubled (from 2.4 to 5.1 per 100,000 population) between 2007 and 2015. This increase marked a forty-year high. The suicide rate for boys in the same age group rose by 31 percent (from 10.8 to 14.2 per 100,000 population) between 2007 and 2015. The suicide rate for teen boys was highest between the mid-1980s and mid-1990s. The CDC report is based on data collected between 1975 and 2015; 2015 is the most recent year for which such figures were available.

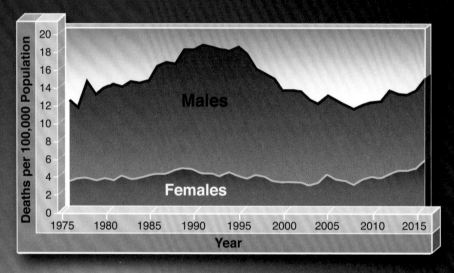

Source: Centers for Disease Control and Prevention, "QuickStats: Suicide Rates for Teens Aged 15–19 Years, by Sex—United States, 1975–2015," August 4, 2017. www.cdc.gov.

A Devastating Impact

Suicide takes the life of one person but affects the lives of many. "Suicide . . . causes immeasurable pain, suffering, and loss to individuals, families, and communities nationwide,"[4] state the Office of the Surgeon General, a federal agency, and the National Action Alliance for Suicide Prevention, a nonprofit organization. Survivors of a loved one who took his or her own life may experience ongoing pain and suffering, including grief, depression, anxiety, post-traumatic stress disorder (PTSD), and increased risk of suicidal thoughts and suicide themselves.

A 2016 study by researchers at the University of Kentucky found that 48 percent of the adult population knew at least one person who died by suicide in their lifetime. The people exposed to suicide were twice as likely to have diagnosable depression as those not exposed, and they were almost twice as likely to have diagnosable anxiety. They also were almost twice as likely to have suicidal thoughts. Those closest to the person who took their life were even more at risk of depression and anxiety. Their odds of having PTSD were almost four times higher than individuals who have not been exposed to suicide.

> "Suicide . . . causes immeasurable pain, suffering, and loss to individuals, families, and communities nationwide."[4]
>
> —Office of the Surgeon General and the National Action Alliance for Suicide Prevention

The Social Costs of Suicide

Most discussions about the effects of suicide focus on the private pain of survivors, but suicide has a social cost as well. Researchers at the Heller School for Social Policy and Management at Brandeis University estimated the cost of US suicides and suicide attempts to be $93.5 billion a year. The vast majority of this cost (97.1 percent) comes from lost productivity.

The researchers estimate that each suicide results in $1.3 million in lost productivity over the course of the person's expected life span. The CDC notes that "the true economic costs are likely higher" because the study did not include "monetary figures related to other societal costs such as those associated with the pain and suffering of family members or other impacts."[5]

What Causes Suicide?

The tremendous emotional and social costs of suicide have driven individuals, communities, and governments to seek ways to prevent it. Effective suicide prevention requires health officials, authorities, and families to understand its cause, but this is a very complex subject. "Suicide, like other human behaviors, has no single determining cause," states the CDC. "Instead, suicide occurs in response to multiple biological, psychological, interpersonal, environmental and societal influences that interact with one another, often over time."[6]

More than 90 percent of people who take their own lives have a mental disorder, either depression, bipolar disorder, or some other diagnosis, according to the National Alliance on Mental Illness. Substance abuse is also a major risk factor for suicide. "Alcohol and drug abuse can worsen thoughts of suicide and make you feel reckless or impulsive enough to act on your thoughts,"[7] states the Mayo Clinic.

Some prescription medications, such as antidepressants, have been linked to an increase in suicidal thoughts or behavior. Having certain medical conditions such as chronic disease, chronic pain, or terminal illness has also been linked to depression and suicidal thinking. Psychological influences can include feelings of hopelessness, worthlessness, agitation, social isolation, or loneliness. Interpersonal factors might include a stressful life event, such as the death of a loved one, a breakup, or financial problems. Environmental risk factors can include having a family history of violence, including physical or sexual abuse.

Teens are subject to the same risk factors as adults, but they also have some that are unique to their age group. These include having a conflict with close friends or family members, being the victim of bullying, being uncertain of their sexual orientation, or hearing an account of suicide or knowing a peer who died by suicide. Being a victim of family violence, including physical or sexual abuse, is also a major risk factor. Being exposed to others people's suicidal behavior, such as that of family members, peers, or even celebrities, can pose a risk to vulnerable teens. In fact, between 1 and 5 percent of teen suicides occur in clusters among kids who know each other, go to the same school, or live in the same community. Mental health experts sometimes refer to this phenomenon as suicide contagion, because it can spread like a contagious disease.

What Can Be Done?

Experts disagree about which of these components are most important, which should be given priority, and how preventive measures can best be implemented by families, schools, health care professionals, and government agencies. For example, research shows that when the media focuses on the suicide of a celebrity, the suicide rate rises, a phenomenon known as the copycat effect. The question is how to handle the problem. Families with at-risk teenagers often think the media should downplay such suicides. Those in the media often say it is up to the family to intervene. Some believe school counseling might be in order. Others think government has a role to play. Similar controversies exist in other areas, including the role of antidepressant medication in suicide; the impact of new technology, including cyberbullying and depression linked to excessive cell phone use; and fictional depictions of suicide. "Suicide is a tragic global public health problem," says Dr. Catherine Le Galès-Camus of WHO. "There is an urgent need for coordinated and intensified global action to prevent this needless toll."[8]

Chapter One

Do Antidepressant Drugs Contribute to the Problem of Teen Suicide?

Antidepressants Contribute to Teen Suicide

- Antidepressants can dangerously affect the balance of chemicals in the brain.
- A person's response to a medication cannot be predicted with certainty.
- Teens who take antidepressants for depression have twice the risk of suicidal thinking and behavior as those who do not.

The Debate at a Glance

Antidepressants Help Prevent Teen Suicide

- The risks of suicide when taking antidepressants have been exaggerated.
- Completed suicides increase when antidepressant use decreases.
- Antidepressants are effective in treating depression, the main cause of suicide.

Antidepressants Contribute to Teen Suicide

"No child emerges from a course of antidepressants unharmed. Even short-term use can result in some permanent damage to the brain."

—Brian, founder of AntiDepAware.

Interview with the author, September 12, 2017.

Consider these questions as you read:

1. Analyze the author's use of the story of Reece Burrowes. Did you find it compelling and good evidence to support the essay's argument? Or did you find it too narrow to be informative about the issue? Explain your reasoning.
2. Consider the various studies put forth in this essay. Which one did you find most compelling or persuasive, and why?
3. In your opinion, is suicidal thinking an acceptable side effect of a medication given to treat depression? If so, why? If not, why not?

Editor's note: The discussion that follows presents common arguments made in support of this perspective, reinforced by facts, quotes, and examples taken from various sources.

Reece Burrowes was a popular seventeen-year-old student who attended Wilmington Grammar School for Boys in Wilmington, England. He enjoyed playing American football and was a running back for the Kent Exiles Youth team, helping them to a third successive divisional title in 2015. The headmaster at Burrowes's school described him as "a quiet, hard-working and extremely popular young man who had achieved very well in his . . . exams and had amazing potential in front of him."[9] That potential, however, went unrealized. On December 6, 2015, Burrowes took his own life. Unbeknownst to his parents, Burrowes had started taking the antidepressant sertraline (known in the United States as Zoloft) six days earlier. His parents believe that instead of helping Burrowes, the antidepressants caused him to take his life.

Two weeks before his death, on November 23, Burrowes went to see a doctor about emotional problems he was having, including doing self-harm to his legs. The doctor, Edwin Lim, later noted that Burrowes said he had "fleeting thoughts about suicide" but did not have plans to end his life. "On the surface he seemed very happy. He couldn't pinpoint anything that was making him unhappy,"[10] Lim testified at an inquest that looked into the young man's death. A week later, Burrowes returned for a follow-up appointment. He was seen by Dr. Jhumur Moir, who told the inquest that Burrowes still had thoughts of self-harm. "Those thoughts were still there, but not suicide,"[11] said Moir. At that visit, Moir gave Burrowes a prescription for sertraline in 50 mg doses. A week later, Burrowes was dead.

Warnings for Teens

According to guidelines published by the National Institute for Health and Care Excellence (NICE), the governing body for health care in England, Burrowes should not have received the antidepressant. According to NICE, the only antidepressant that can be prescribed for teens is fluoxetine (also known by the brand name Prozac). In addition, sertraline should only be given for moderate to severe clinical depression, which Burrowes had not been diagnosed with. Finally, the prescription should only be made after at least three months of interpersonal therapy, or counseling, and if the counseling has shown to be ineffective—but Burrowes had never received such counseling.

NICE created its antidepressant guidelines after a 2004 review of drug trials in the United Kingdom found increased suicidal behavior in children and adolescents up to age eighteen. This study resulted in serious warnings against these drugs being used in this age group.

At about the same time as the NICE study, the FDA was concluding its own review of twenty-two hundred children treated with such

The Link Between Antidepressants and Teen Suicide Is Growing

In a 2017 study, researcher Jan Larsson reviewed the toxicological (blood and tissue) reports of women age fifteen to twenty-four who had committed suicide in Sweden. Larson found that the presence of antidepressants in toxicology reports has increased over the last fifteen years for which data is available, from 13 percent of the cases in 1999 to 41 percent of the cases in 2013. The study shows that a higher percentage of teens and young adults who take their lives have antidepressants in their bloodstream when they do so.

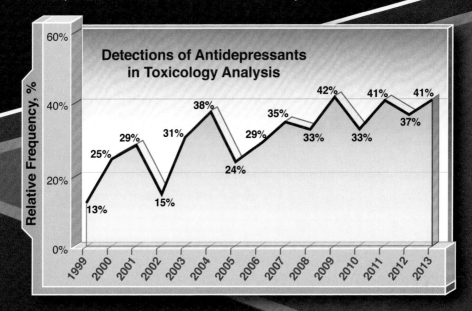

Source: Jan Larsson, "Antidepressants and Suicide Among Young Women in Sweden 1999–2013," *International Journal of Risk & Safety in Medicine*, September 1, 2017. http://content.iospress.com.

medications. The FDA found that about 4 percent of minors taking antidepressants exhibited suicidal thinking, and some attempted suicide. This was twice the rate of suicidality (suicidal thinking and behavior) of the patients who were given a medication-free pill known as a placebo.

Based on these findings, the FDA required antidepressant makers to include a strong warning on their products regarding suicide-related side effects. The FDA warning advised doctors to monitor young patients for any signs that their symptoms were worsening, any unusual changes in behavior, and any indications that they were suicidal, especially during the first few months of treatment and after dose changes. This warning is significant, because suicidal thoughts—known as suicide ideation—almost always come before suicide. If antidepressants increase the risk of suicide ideation, they also increase the risk of suicide.

How Antidepressants Work

The body produces many chemicals that enable brain cells to function properly, and some of these chemicals affect mood and behavior. An imbalance of these chemicals can cause mental disorders, such as depression. Antidepressants work by changing the chemistry in a patient's brain. One class of antidepressants, known as selective serotonin reuptake inhibitors, or SSRIs, targets a chemical known as serotonin. Serotonin is a chemical created by the human body that carries signals along and between nerves. It is believed to be especially active in regulating body processes and contributing to feelings of well-being and happiness. By preventing serotonin from being reabsorbed in the brain (a process known as reuptake), SSRIs make more serotonin available to brain cells. By increasing the amount of serotonin in the brain, these drugs can alleviate the symptoms of depression, helping the patient feel better.

> "Teen bodies do not absorb and eliminate drugs in the same way adult bodies do, and their brains may be affected differently as well."[12]
>
> —The *Harvard Mental Health Letter*

The problem with antidepressants, as with any drug, is that they do not work the same way for every patient. Each person's brain and body are unique, and a drug that works well for one person may not work well for another. This is particularly true regarding drugs that alter brain chemistry, known as psychotropic drugs. The brain is extremely sensitive, and small changes in its chemistry can cause big changes in mood and behavior. "Teen bodies do not absorb and eliminate drugs in the same way adult bodies do, and their brains may be affected differently as well," states the *Harvard Mental Health Letter*. "A child's development could be detoured [harmed] by a misapplication of drugs."[12]

Unintended and unwanted changes are known as side effects. Common side effects of SSRI antidepressants include drowsiness, nausea, insomnia, nervousness, dizziness, and increased agitation or restlessness. Side effects can also include suicidal thoughts and behavior, especially among teens. "An individual's response to a medication cannot be predicted with certainty," states the National Institute of Mental Health (NIMH), discussing fluoxetine, the only SSRI approved for use by the FDA for teens. This unpredictability poses a grave risk. "Fluoxetine can be helpful in treating childhood depression, and can lead to significant improvement of depression overall. However, it may increase the risk for suicidal behaviors in a small subset of adolescents."[13]

An Underestimated Danger

Many experts who have studied the problem of teen suicide believe that NICE and the FDA have actually understated the dangers inherent in antidepressant use. David Healy, professor of psychiatry at Bangor University in North Wales, is one of them. "There are probably up to an extra 2,500 suicides in Europe triggered by an SSRI antidepressant,"[14] Healy said in an interview with BBC television.

This idea is supported by a 2016 study by the Nordic Cochrane Centre in Copenhagen, Denmark, which found that antidepressants are more dangerous than drug companies and government regulators suggest. The researchers reviewed seventy antidepressant drug trials that involved 18,526 subjects—the largest-ever analysis of antidepressant trials. The study found that the original drug trials excluded many suicides, suicide attempts, and instances of suicide ideation from the final reports to the government, for a variety of reasons. Discussing the research in an editorial for the *BMJ*, a medical journal, Joanna Moncrieff, a senior lecturer in psychiatry at University College London, wrote, "New evidence from clinical study reports reveals misclassification, misrepresentation, and under-reporting of serious harm."[15]

When the additional suicidal events were taken into account, the researchers found the risk of suicidality in patients under eighteen receiving antidepressants was twice as high as the risk for patients given a placebo. This greatly concerned the researchers, who recommended that such drugs' use in teens be reconsidered. "We suggest minimal use of antidepressants in children, adolescents, and young adults, as the serious harms seem to be greater, and as their effect seems to be below what is clinically relevant,"[16] the researchers wrote. Peter C. Gøtzsche, the study's lead author, was even blunter in his comments to the London *Telegraph*. "Antidepressants don't work in children, that is pretty clear," he said. "What I get out of this colossal underreporting of suicides is that SSRIs likely increase suicides in all ages."[17]

> "What I get out of this colossal underreporting of suicides is that SSRIs likely increase suicides in all ages."[17]
>
> —Peter C. Gøtzsche, professor, University of Copenhagen

Unfortunately for Reece Burrowes, the new research about the dangers of antidepressants came too late for him and his family. Reece's mother, Tracy, writes on a suicide prevention website: "I strongly believe that Reece would still be with us if the doctor hadn't prescribed Sertraline 50mg when all that Reece needed was counselling to get through everyday teenage problems."[18] Knowing that antidepressants can actually increase the risk of suicide will enable doctors, parents, and patients to make sure that no other teen succumbs to the same fate as Reece.

Antidepressants Help Prevent Teen Suicide

"Untreated depression can be lethal to adolescents. For many, medication is a lifeline."

—Harold S. Koplewicz, founding president of the Child Mind Institute

Harold S. Koplewicz, "Antidepressants and Teen Suicides," Child Mind Institute, January 9, 2017. https://childmind.org.

Consider these questions as you read:

1. Do you think the media exaggerated the importance of the FDA's warning about the side effects of antidepressants? Explain your answer.
2. Does the fact that suicide attempts went up when antidepressant prescriptions went down prove that antidepressants help prevent suicide? Why or why not?
3. If you were a parent, would you allow your child to take antidepressants if doctors prescribed them? Explain your answer.

Editor's note: The discussion that follows presents common arguments made in support of this perspective, reinforced by facts, quotes, and examples taken from various sources.

In 2004 the FDA proposed that makers of antidepressant medications warn doctors and patients that an increased risk of suicidal thinking was a possible side effect among teens and young adults who took the drugs. The warning is known as a black box warning because it is printed in bold, framed type at the top of the paper inserts that come with medications. It is the strongest type of warning the FDA can issue.

The FDA's warning set off alarms across the country. "F.D.A. links drugs to being suicidal,"[19] blared a headline in the *New York Times*. "FDA confirms antidepressants raise children's suicide risk,"[20] declared

Antidepressants Help Control Suicide Triggers in Teens

Teens experiencing major depressive episodes are at extremely high risk for suicide. For many of these teens, antidepressants combined with psychotherapy are an effective way to treat depression. The combination of therapy and medication can help seriously depressed teens learn to recognize common suicide triggers and explore how to deal with them in the future.

How Antidepressants Can Help

- Improve mood
- Improve appetite
- Increase focus
- Resolve sleep disturbance associated with depression
- Decrease anxious symptoms that can occur with depression
- Decrease depressive symptoms that can trigger suicidal thoughts

Source: Katie Hurley, "Teen Depression: The Pros and Cons of Medication," PsyCom, July 10, 2017. www.psycom.net.

the *Washington Post*. These headlines were extremely misleading, however. The study that prompted the FDA warning found a tiny increase in suicidal *thoughts* among a small number of patients but no increase at all in actual suicides. This is because not only do antidepressants *not* cause suicide, but they are sometimes the only thing working to prevent it.

An Imprecise, Overblown Warning

The FDA based its warning on a review of clinical data on twenty-two hundred children who had been treated with SSRIs. It found a 4 percent increase in "suicide thinking and behavior" among those age eighteen to twenty-four during the first two months of treatment with the drugs. However, the FDA did not find any completed suicides among the twenty-two hundred patients it studied. "Nobody died and nobody killed themselves,"[21] observes Dr. Gene Beresin, executive director of the Clay Center for Young Healthy Minds. Many doctors criticized the FDA's handling of the warning. "There were enough reports of suicide attempts among young people starting an SSRI to justify the warning," writes Dr. Howard LeWine, chief medical editor of Harvard Health Publications. "But the FDA could have done a much better job of explaining that this *did not* mean that taking SSRIs *caused* more suicide attempts."[22]

The FDA also made a mistake by extending its warning to all antidepressants. At the time of the black box warning against antidepressants, the FDA had approved only three SSRIs for use by children and teens: Prozac (fluoxetine), Zoloft (sertraline), and fluvoxamine maleate. All three drugs were approved for the treatment of obsessive-compulsive disorder. Only Prozac was approved for use in children and adolescents to treat major depressive disorder. Nevertheless, the FDA studied nine antidepressants and extended its warning to all antidepressants.

Unaware of the facts, patients and parents worried about the potentially fatal side effects reported in the media. As a result of the uproar, many physicians stopped prescribing antidepressants for teens and young adults. However, this was a disaster, because it left many patients without effective treatment. "[This] led a lot of parents to be terrified to have their children on these medications—and they took them off and there was a lot of untreated, serious depression,"[23] says Robert D. Gibbons, a University of Chicago biostatistician who advised the FDA on the issue.

Fewer Antidepressants, More Suicide Attempts

Indeed, the FDA warnings had the opposite effect of what was intended. Consider the findings of a 2014 Harvard Medical School study, which reviewed more than 7 million health care records from before, during, and after the time that the FDA warnings were issued (2000–2010). Specifically, the study examined the records of about 1.1 million adolescents and 1.4 million young adults. To no one's surprise, the researchers found that antidepressant use declined sharply after the warning. Yet the researchers found that as the use of antidepressants decreased, the number of suicide attempts increased. Suicide attempts increased 22 percent among adolescents and 34 percent among young adults in the two years after the warnings were issued. "Our study provides the first evidence that suicide attempts increased rather than decreased after the warnings,"[24] write the researchers. Clearly, antidepressants had been working, because when patients went off the drugs, the number of suicide attempts increased.

The media did not report the increase in suicide attempts as loudly and persistently as it did the FDA warning. Many experts found the lack of attention to the facts to be disgraceful. "If an infection, asthma, or heart condition increased 30 percent over the last decade, the public would go ballistic," Beresin told ABC News. "The FDA would have been under massive attack from all sectors of the population."[25] Instead, the 2014 Harvard study findings went largely unnoticed, and more teens remained at risk because they were not receiving the medication they needed.

> "If the intent of the pediatric black box warning was to save lives, the warning failed, and in fact it may have had the opposite effect; more children and adolescents have committed suicide since it was introduced."[26]
>
> Robert D. Gibbons, director of the Center for Health Statistics at the University of Chicago

Antidepressants Were Working

Tragically, the FDA's warning cost lives. According to researchers at the University of Chicago Center for Health Statistics, not only did suicide attempts increase after the FDA's warning, but so too did completed suicides. The researchers examined SSRI prescriptions for children and adolescents in both the United States and the Netherlands immediately after the warnings issued by the FDA and its counterpart in Europe. The researchers found that after the warnings, antidepressant prescriptions for youths decreased in both countries (by approximately 22 percent).

At the same time, suicide rates went up—by 49 percent in the Netherlands (from 2003 to 2005) and by 14 percent in the United States (from 2003 to 2004). Regarding the increase in the United States, it was the largest year-to-year increase in suicide rates for that age group since the CDC began systematically collecting suicide statistics in 1979. "If the intent of the pediatric black box warning was to save lives, the warning failed, and in fact it may have had the opposite effect; more children and adolescents have committed suicide since it was introduced,"[26] wrote Gibbons, the study's lead author. Clearly, antidepressant treatments had been saving lives, and the sudden decrease in their use resulted in an increase in suicides.

The Benefits of Antidepressants Outweigh Their Risks

Antidepressants are no more dangerous than a sugar pill, but they can successfully treat several mental disorders. Researchers at Ohio State University reviewed the results of antidepressant drug trials that compared the effects of antidepressants and placebos, which are sugar pills that do not contain any medication. They found a slight increase in suicidal thinking among those who took both the real and the fake medications but the differences were so small that they were not significant. However, they found that the antidepressants effectively treated depressive disorder, obsessive-compulsive disorder, and anxiety disorders. As a result, the researchers found that the benefits of antidepressants outweighed the risks to children and adolescents with serious depression and anxiety. "Benefits of antidepressants appear to be much greater than risks from suicidal ideation [and] suicide attempt across indications,"[27] they wrote.

> "For many children and teens, antidepressants are an effective way to treat depression, anxiety, obsessive-compulsive disorder or other mental health conditions."[28]
>
> —Mayo Clinic

This is why many physicians and health care organizations stand behind the use of antidepressants to treat mental disorders and prevent suicide. This includes the Mayo Clinic, which states, "For many children and teens, antidepressants are an effective way to treat depression, anxiety, obsessive-compulsive disorder or other mental health conditions."[28] Harold S. Koplewicz, a doctor who founded the nonprofit organization Child Mind Institute, agrees. "Over 90 percent of all young people who commit suicide are suffering from severe mental illness," says Koplewicz. "Should we prescribe these medications to young people? The answer, I believe, is absolutely yes."[29]

Chapter Two

Is the Media Contributing to the Rise in Teen Suicide?

The Media Glamorizes Suicide

- Internet searches regarding suicide spike after popular depictions of the act.
- Media that glamorizes suicide serves to normalize the act, which makes it more common.
- The media's coverage of high-profile suicides is followed by increased suicide rates, known as a copycat effect.

The Debate at a Glance

The Media Reflects an Existing Trend in Teen Suicide

- Artists and the media respond to trends; they do not make them.
- Portrayals of suicide in the media can prompt a surge in suicide prevention Internet searches, rather than copycat searches.
- People often scapegoat the media because doing so is easier than addressing the real causes of suicide.

The Media Glamorizes Suicide

"Dramatic and detailed portrayals of suicide needlessly put vulnerable young people at risk of copycat behavior as they see how to carry out harmful or potentially fatal acts."

—Dr. Helen Rayner, a psychiatrist specializing in children and adolescent mental health

Quoted in Denis Campbell, "Netflix Show Condemned for 'Romanticising' Teenager's Suicide," *Guardian* (Manchester), April 21, 2017. www.theguardian.com.

Consider these questions as you read:

1. After reading this essay, are you convinced that Internet searches mirror real-world suicide rates? Why or why not?
2. To what extent do you think books and movies can affect the behavior of people? Explain your reasoning and provide evidence from the texts you have read in your answer.
3. How powerful do you think the copycat effect is when it comes to something serious like suicide? Explain your answer.

Editor's note: The discussion that follows presents common arguments made in support of this perspective, reinforced by facts, quotes, and examples taken from various sources.

On the last day of March 2017, Netflix released *13 Reasons Why*, a thirteen-episode television series chronicling the life and death of teenager Hannah Baker, who is shown taking her life in the final episode. The program was incredibly popular. Fans mentioned it 11 million times on the social networking platform Twitter over the first three weeks of April, making it the most-tweeted-about program of 2017. The makers of the program believed this was a good thing, because it brought the issue of teen suicide—often a taboo subject—into the open. "Our members tell us that *13 Reasons Why* has helped spark important conversations in their families and communities around the world,"[30] Netflix said in a statement. This is just a smoke screen, however. Research shows that the program is just the latest piece in a long line of media events to glamorize suicide and trigger real-life suicides.

Measurable Effects

The show's devastating effects are evident in data collected immediately after the series was released. Researchers from five American universities used Google Trends to analyze search engine queries in the nineteen days following the show's release. What they found was chilling. During that period, there were between 900,000 and 1.5 million more searches than usual for words and phrases related to suicide. For example, searches of the phrase "how to commit suicide" were up 26 percent, "commit suicide" was up 18 percent, and "how to kill yourself" was up 9 percent. In addition, searches for precise suicide methods increased after the series' release. The researchers found this data particularly disturbing because, as they wrote, "Suicide research trends are correlated with actual suicides."[31]

> "I see this troubling data as a strong call to action. The show must be taken down."[32]
>
> —John W. Ayers, professor of public health at San Diego State University

John W. Ayers, a professor of public health at San Diego State University and a coauthor of the study, thought the correlation was strong enough to justify taking the series off the air. He said research shows that when Internet searches about suicide increase, so do actual suicides. "Suicide rates have likely gone up as a result of this program," says Ayers. "For me, as a data-driven public health scientist, I see this troubling data as a strong call to action. The show must be taken down."[32]

Normalizing Suicide

Ayers and his colleagues predicted that the media's glamorization of suicide would lead to actual suicide attempts and suicides, and this is exactly what psychiatrists, psychologists, and counselors reported seeing in their patients after *13 Reasons Why* was released. Some of the patients even admitted that they were copying what they saw on TV. For example, a twelve-year-old girl who attempted suicide in May 2017 told Dan Nelson, medical director of the child psychiatry inpatient unit at Cincinnati Children's Hospital, that *13 Reasons Why* had influenced her. "She said to me, 'I saw that show and it really convinced me that suicide was a normal thing to do.'" Nelson was shocked. "I've never heard that," he says. "In 30 years, I've never heard a child say this thing made me think suicide is normal." Kimberly O'Brien, a researcher at Boston Children's Hospital and an instructor in psychiatry at Harvard Medical School, observed the same phenomenon. "I personally have seen multiple psychiatric admissions where the admission note details the fact that the teen said that they wanted to 'kill myself the way the girl in *13 Reason Why* did,'"[33] says O'Brien.

> "She said to me, 'I saw that show and it really convinced me that suicide was a normal thing to do.'"[33]
>
> —Dan Nelson, medical director of the child psychiatry inpatient unit at Cincinnati Children's Hospital

Unfortunately, the show inspired not only suicide attempts but completed suicides. California teen Bella Herndon took her own life in April 2017, just days after watching *13 Reasons Why*. So did Priscilla Chui, another California teen who took her life that month. Chui's family says the show acted as a trigger for her. "It's very graphic," says Peter Chui, Priscilla's uncle. "I feel it's dangerous for that small percentage of young adults who the show can become a trigger for them and I feel as if the show gives only one alternative for cyber bullying and other teenage issues."[34]

The Werther Effect

The idea that a prominent suicide—actual or fictional—can trigger others is not new. In 1774 Johann Wolfgang von Goethe published *The Sorrows of Young Werther*, a novel in which the main character took his life in an emotionally charged scene. The book was extremely popular, and a number of young men across Europe ended their lives via the same

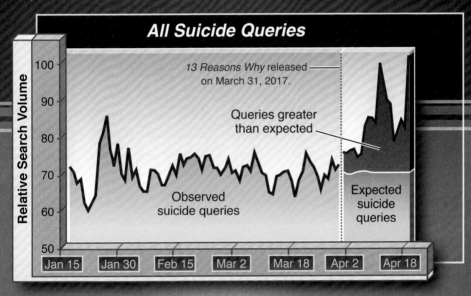

Suicide Queries Rise Dramatically After Relase of *13 Reasons Why*

Researchers analyzed suicide-related queries in Google before and after the March 31, 2017, release of *13 Reasons Why*, a television series that included a graphic depiction of a teen suicide. The number of suicide-related queries went up dramatically after the program's release (represented by the dotted blue line). The shaded area represents the number of queries that were greater than expected, based on the average of the previous eleven weeks. This shows the impact the media can have on suicidal thinking.

All Suicide Queries

Relative Search Volume

100
90
80
70
60
50

13 Reasons Why released on March 31, 2017.

Queries greater than expected

Observed suicide queries

Expected suicide queries

Jan 15 Jan 30 Feb 15 Mar 2 Mar 18 Apr 2 Apr 18

Source: John W. Ayers et al., "Internet Searches for Suicide Following the Release of *13 Reasons Why*," *JAMA Internal Medicine*, July 31, 2017. http://jamanetwork.com.

method, and dressed in the same way, as Goethe's character; some even died with the novel open to the page describing the suicide.

While the exact number of these suicides is not known, modern researchers have shown that high-profile suicides are often followed by an increase in the suicide rate for a short time—a phenomenon they have dubbed the Werther effect, after Goethe's novel. This term was coined by David Phillips, a sociology professor at the University of California–San

Diego, in a landmark 1974 research paper in which he and colleagues compared twenty years of nationally collected suicide data to front-page news stories about suicides during the same time period. Phillips found that twenty-seven out of the thirty-three front-page suicides were followed by increases in suicide rates. Each increase lasted for about two months. "[We] were the first to provide modern large scale evidence that there is in fact such a thing as copycat suicide,"[35] says Phillips.

One of the most powerful examples of the Werther effect occurred in 1962, when the famous actress Marilyn Monroe took her own life at age thirty-six. For days news about Monroe's death, often accompanied by pictures of the glamorous star, were featured on the front pages of newspapers, in magazines, and on television news. One of the most sensationalized suicides in history, Monroe's death on August 5, 1962, was followed by 303 more suicides that month, a 12 percent increase in the suicide rate.

The Werther effect, as originally noted, has been shown to follow fictional portrayals of suicidal behavior—and not just *13 Reasons Why*. For example, a 1999 episode of the BBC One hospital drama series *Casualty* depicted a fictional Royal Air Force pilot who took an overdose of an over-the-counter medication in an attempt to end his life. Researchers from Oxford University found that episodes of self-poisoning increased by 17 percent in the first week after the broadcast and by 9 percent in the second week. The connection was not a coincidence. Twenty percent of the interviewed patients admitted that the show had influenced their behavior.

The Copycat Problem

Media reports about the suicides of people who are not famous can also trigger other suicides, especially if the descriptions of the suicides are sensationalized. For example, in 1983 a man in Vienna, Austria, tried to kill himself by jumping in front of a subway train. He survived, and several newspapers covered the story in detail. The following year seven more people killed themselves by jumping into the subway, and the local newspapers ran graphic stories about each one. In 1985 thirteen people attempted suicide in this way, and ten died. The subway suicides continued, reaching a peak in 1987, when twenty-two people attempted suicide, half of whom lived and half of whom died.

Desperate to prevent more suicides, the Austrian branch of the International Association for Suicide Prevention pleaded with the press to tone down the reporting. The group issued a series of guidelines, including not showing grieving family members and not using the word *suicide* in headlines. Local news media followed the recommendations—and they worked. "The number of suicides and suicide attempts on the Viennese subway decreased by nearly 80 percent,"[36] reports Thomas Niederkrotenthaler, an assistant professor at the Medical University of Vienna.

The documented connection between the media and suicide is so strong that in 2008 the World Health Organization issued an eighteen-page guidebook for members of the media, titled *Preventing Suicide: A Resource for Media Professionals*, in an attempt to tone down media reports and prevent future suicides. Producers of shows like *13 Reasons Why* would do well to read this guide, because research shows that the media can influence people and change lives. As a member of the community, the media has a responsibility to avoid putting young lives in danger by glamorizing suicide.

The Media Reflects an Existing Trend in Teen Suicide

"There is little empirical evidence that demonstrates that fictional representations [of suicide] directly lead to copy-cat behavior."

—William Proctor, a journalism lecturer at Bournemouth University in England

William Proctor, "Open Letter to Journalists, Mental Health Campaigners and Psychologists," Bournemouth University, May 25, 2017. www1.bournemouth.ac.uk.

Consider these questions as you read:

1. In your opinion, should artists avoid dramatizing controversial subjects if there is a danger of causing harm? Why or why not?
2. How persuasive is the argument that it is easy to blame the media for suicides but hard to know how many lives it saves? Explain your answer.
3. What are some of the reasons people might have for attacking or scapegoating the media regarding suicide? Give examples.

Editor's note: The discussion that follows presents common arguments made in support of this perspective, reinforced by facts, quotes, and examples taken from various sources.

Within hours of its release on March 31, 2017, the Netflix series *13 Reasons Why*, a drama that explores the topic of teen suicide, was on its way to being the most talked-about program of the year. More than six hundred thousand articles were soon written about the program, and tens of millions of people were discussing it on social media. This was a good thing—the more people discuss the issue of teen suicide, the better the chances of understanding it and saving lives. Unfortunately, some of the loudest voices discussing the program are condemning it for increasing the risk of real-life suicides. This view is wrong. Books, movies, and television programs do not set trends; they reflect them.

A Trend That Already Existed

According to the CDC, the suicide rate among teenage girls reached a forty-year high in 2015. In fact, the suicide rates among teen girls doubled between 2007 and 2015. The fictional portrayal of the suicide of Hannah Baker, the teenage main character of *13 Reasons Why*, reflects this horrific reality.

Aware of the rising number of teen suicides, Selena Gomez, the producer of the show, wanted to start a national conversation on suicide. "It is uncomfortable for people to talk about, but it is happening," says Gomez, "and hopefully [*13 Reasons Why*] opened the door for people to actually accept what's happening and actually go and change it, talk about it."[37] Author Nic Sheff, who once tried to take his own life and who served as a writer and story editor for the series, was drawn to work on the project for the same reason. As he told *Vanity Fair*:

> As soon as I read the pilot for *13 Reasons Why*, I immediately knew it was a project I wanted to be involved in. I was struck by how relevant and even necessary a show like this was: offering hope to young people, letting them know that they are not alone—that somebody out there gets them. . . . I recognized the potential for the show to bravely and unflinchingly explore the realities of suicide for teens and young adults—a topic I felt very strongly about.[38]

Sparking Interest in Suicide Prevention

To the extent that the makers of *13 Reasons Why* wanted to spark interest in the topic, they succeeded. Not only is the series the most tweeted-about television program of the year, but a study published in *JAMA Internal Medicine* found that there was a 19 percent increase in search engine queries about suicide on Google in the nineteen days following the series' release.

Detractors of the program—including one of the scientists who co-authored the study—have used this data to argue that the series caused an increase in suicidal thoughts and suicide itself. What they leave out is that the research clearly shows that the program sparked more queries about suicide *prevention* than it did about suicide ideation or methods. For example, the largest increases were found in what the researchers called "public awareness indicative searches."[39] These search terms included "teen suicide," which was up 34 percent, and "suicide prevention," up 23 percent. Queries for suicide hotlines were also higher, including "suicide hotline number," up 21 percent, and "suicide hotline," up 12 percent. Netflix found the results of the study encouraging. "We always believed this show would increase discussion around this tough subject matter," the company said in a statement. "This is an interesting quasi-experimental study that confirms this."[40]

> "I was struck by how relevant and even necessary a show like this was: offering hope to young people, letting them know that they are not alone—that somebody out there gets them."[38]
>
> —Nic Sheff, author and story editor for *13 Reasons Why*

Cause or Coincidence?

The authors of the search engine study did also find an increase in searches for topics related to suicidal thoughts. However, the researchers cautioned against making too much of this fact. As they wrote, "It is unclear whether any query preceded an actual suicide attempt."[41] Relatives of two teens who took their lives shortly after watching *13 Reasons Why* claim the series triggered the girls' suicides. This is possible—and would be tragic—but it is by no means certain. The causes of suicide are extremely complex, and these teens might have carried out their suicides even in the absence of the series. John Herndon, the father of one of the teens, Bella Herndon, said his daughter had been bullied since middle school. The family of the other teen, Priscilla Chui, said she had been treated for depression long before the series had been released. "It's unlikely that

Suicide Was Increasing Even Before the Release of *13 Reasons Why*

In 2016 the Centers for Disease Control and Prevention (CDC) reported that suicide (red line) had surpassed homicide (purple line) to become the second-leading cause of death of people between the ages of fifteen and nineteen, behind only accidents (green line). The teenage suicide rate increased from 8 deaths per 100,000 in 1999 to 8.7 deaths per 100,000 in 2014. This shows that suicides were already on the rise before the release of *13 Reasons Why*, a reality that the makers of the program wanted to dramatize.

Suicide Surpassed Homicide to Become Second-Leading Cause of Death for Teenagers, Age 15–19, in the United States

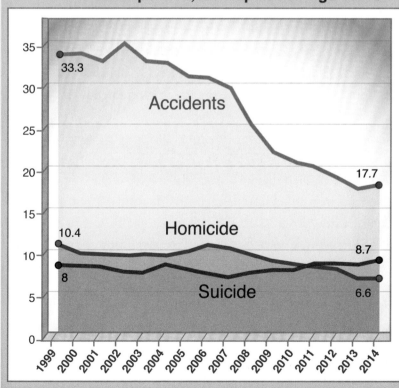

Deaths per 100,000 Population Age 15–19

Accidents: 33.3 ... 17.7

Homicide: 10.4 ... 6.6

Suicide: 8 ... 8.7

Source: Alicia VanOrman and Beth Jarosz, "Suicide Replaces Homicides as Second-Leading Cause of Death Among U.S. Teenagers," Population Reference Bureau, June 2016. www.prb.org.

one show alone could trigger someone to attempt suicide,"[42] says Eric Beeson, a licensed professional counselor who serves as an online faculty member at the Family Institute at Northwestern University.

It is also possible that the series directly or indirectly saved lives. This is difficult to know, because unlike suicides, saved lives are impossible to count. However, each episode of *13 Reasons Why* carried a "mature audience" advisory warning, and the three most graphic episodes—including the final one that depicted the suicide—included additional warnings with links to suicide prevention websites and a hotline. It is entirely possible that one of these warnings or some of the Google search queries prompted by the series led to hotline calls that saved lives.

As a public service, Netflix also created a thirty-minute documentary, "Beyond the Reasons," as a companion to the series. The program includes not only the show's cast and producers, but also mental health experts. They discuss some of the difficult issues raised by the series, including bullying, depression, sexual assault, and suicide. The *13 Reasons Why* suicide was intentionally portrayed in a way to turn viewers *off* to suicide—to make them realize how utterly futile an act it really is. In the documentary, Brian Yorkey, the series creator, explained that he wanted the suicide scene "to be painful to watch because we wanted it to be very clear that there is nothing—in any way—worthwhile about suicide."[43] Many people thought the show accomplished its aims. Dawn Zawadzki, a paralegal from Fort Mill, South Carolina, watched part of the series with her sixteen-year-old daughter. "Everybody is saying 'it glamorizes suicide,' but I don't think it does," says Zawadzki. "It's making us wake up and look at it."[44]

> "Everybody is saying '[*13 Reasons Why*] glamorizes suicide,' but I don't think it does. It's making us wake up and look at it."[44]
>
> —Dawn Zawadzki, a paralegal, parent, and viewer of *13 Reasons Why*

Scapegoating the Media

13 Reasons Why is not the first piece of work to be blamed for triggering suicides. As long ago as the 1700s, authorities in Austria, Denmark, and individual cities across Europe banned Johann Wolfgang von Goethe's novel *The Sorrows of Young Werther* because of the so-called Werther fever that was supposedly causing young men to kill themselves in the same way Goethe's character had. A more contemporary example comes from 2014, when the Academy of Motion Picture Arts and Sciences was criticized for posting a tweet that said, "Genie, you're free"[45] after actor Robin Williams committed suicide. Williams had been the voice of Genie in Disney's 1992 film *Aladdin*, and critics claimed the academy's tweet portrayed his suicide in a positive or romanticized light. Such attacks on the media are common because it is easier to blame an external force for suicide than it is to probe into the complex psychological factors that are its actual causes.

Twenty-one academics from around the world, including those in the United Kingdom, France, Portugal, and Peru, believe that *13 Reasons Why* is being scapegoated in this way. They signed an open letter that criticizes journalists, mental health campaigners, and psychologists for "whipping up a moral panic" about the Netflix series. "Many UK presses are giving prime space to certain kinds of voices, many of which are scapegoating the series as 'dangerous,' 'harmful', 'romanticized' and 'sensationalist,'" wrote William Proctor, a journalism lecturer at Bournemouth University in England, on behalf of the group. The signatories to the letter dismissed the search engine study linking *13 Reasons Why* and suicide as bad science. "We can call this the 'media harm theory,'" wrote Proctor. "However, in academic disciplines such as Film, Television, Journalism, Media and Cultural Studies, this approach has been deemed too reductive [and] simplistic."[46]

Proctor is exactly right. Scapegoating books, plays, movies, and television series can draw attention away from the real factors that contribute to suicide. Instead of blaming the media, we should use them to launch serious—and potentially life-saving—discussions about suicide.

Chapter Three

Do New Technologies Contribute to Teen Suicide?

Technology Is Contributing to Teen Suicide

- Cyberbullying has directly led to many teen suicides.
- Social media amplifies embarrassing moments and can lead to suicidal thoughts.
- The pressures of social media are destabilizing vulnerable teens.

The Debate at a Glance

Technology Can Help Prevent Teen Suicide

- Technology has not been shown to cause suicidal behavior.
- Technology can be used to prevent cyberbullying and other ills that contribute to suicide.
- Suicide prevention apps can better connect teens to the help they need.

Technology Is Contributing to Teen Suicide

"Teens who spend three hours a day or more on electronic devices are 35 percent more likely to have a risk factor for suicide, such as making a suicide plan."

—Jean M. Twenge, professor of psychology at San Diego State University

Jean M. Twenge, "Have Smartphones Destroyed a Generation?," *Atlantic*, September 2017. www.theatlantic.com.

Consider these questions as you read:

1. Approximately how many hours a day do you use social media? Overall, how would you say it makes you feel? Bored? Depressed? Connected? Excited? Explain your answer using examples from your personal experience.
2. Do you or anyone you know ever feel anxious about the number of social media "likes" a post receives? If so, what kind of post was it (a photo, a "share," or a comment)? If not, why not?
3. Do you think external factors such as technology contribute to suicide? Why or why not?

Editor's note: The discussion that follows presents common arguments made in support of this perspective, reinforced by facts, quotes, and examples taken from various sources.

In December 2016 eighteen-year-old Brandy Vela of Texas City, Texas, sent a text to her older sister, Jacqueline. It read, "I love you so much just remember that please and I'm so sorry for everything." Knowing that her younger sister had been relentlessly bullied online, Jacqueline called their parents and grandparents and rushed home. "I was the first one here," Jacqueline remembers. "I ran upstairs and I looked in her room and she's against the wall and she has a gun pointed at her chest and she's

just crying and crying and I'm like, 'Brandy please don't, Brandy no.'"
Brandy's parents and grandparents arrived, and everyone pleaded with
the young woman not to end her life. Moments later, Brandy pulled the
trigger. "I was in my parents' room and I just heard the shot and my dad
just yelled, 'Help me, help me, help me,'"[47] Jacqueline recalls. Brandy
was rushed to a local hospital, where she was pronounced dead.

Cyberbullying: A Disturbing Trend

Brandy Vela did not fit the typical profile of a suicidal teen. She was not
suffering from depression or any other mental illness. She was not ad-
dicted to drugs or alcohol. She had not been raped or physically abused.
Her family was stable, and she was popular at school. Brandy did have a
problem, though, and everyone knew what it was. She was being bullied
—relentlessly, horrifically bullied. Her tormenters did not harass her to
her face but instead used technology to taunt her, a practice known as cyberbullying. They sent a barrage of ugly text messages to her cell phone,
created fake Facebook accounts to mock her, and used her picture to
create fake profiles on dating websites, offering sex to strangers. "They
would say, 'I'm a slut and I'm a hoe. Anybody hit me up,'" Jacqueline
says. "It also had her phone number, so she would get text messages and
phone calls all the time. It kept her up at night."[48]

Brandy did everything victims of bullying are advised to do. She notified school officials, changed her phone number, and had her parents
contact various law enforcement agencies—not once but several times.
Police investigated, but the app being used for the messaging was not
traceable. No arrests were made, and the cyberbullying continued. Brandy reported the fake Facebook pages, and they were taken down, but new
ones popped up in their place. It was too much for the teen to handle.
"I can't do this anymore," Brandy told her family moments before she
ended her life. "I'm tired."[49]

The circumstances leading to Brandy Vela's tragic death are part of
a trend. According to a study by the National Center for Telehealth and
Technology, 20 percent to 40 percent of teens have reported being the
victim of cyberbullying at some point in their lives. A 2017 study of

Cyberbullying Is a Gateway to Suicidal Thinking

According to an online forum aimed at stopping cyberbullying through education and counseling, 42 percent of youth report having been cyberbullied, and 20 percent of those adolescents have thought about suicide. This is one way in which technology is contributing to an increase in suicide and suicidal thoughts among teens.

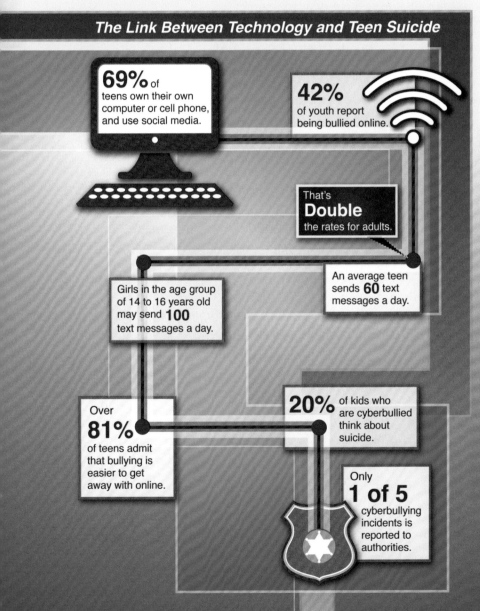

The Link Between Technology and Teen Suicide

69% of teens own their own computer or cell phone, and use social media.

42% of youth report being bullied online.

That's **Double** the rates for adults.

An average teen sends **60** text messages a day.

Girls in the age group of 14 to 16 years old may send **100** text messages a day.

Over **81%** of teens admit that bullying is easier to get away with online.

20% of kids who are cyberbullied think about suicide.

Only **1 of 5** cyberbullying incidents is reported to authorities.

Source: NoBullying.com, "Bullying Suicide Statsics," October 13, 2016. https://nobullying.com.

33,038 middle school students found that being the victim of bullying is a risk factor for depression, psychosis, and suicide ideation and attempts. Researchers at Yale School of Medicine have found that bullying victims are two to nine times more likely to report suicidal thoughts than other adolescents are. Similarly, a study conducted by Florida Atlantic University found that victims of cyberbullying were almost two times as likely to attempt suicide as those who were not.

The Dark Side of Social Networking

Unfortunately, technology exaggerates bad feelings even when bullies are not involved. When someone makes a mistake or does something embarrassing, it can spread quickly via social media. "If something gets said that's hurtful or humiliating, it's not just the kid who said it who knows, it's the entire school or class," says Marsha Levy-Warren, a clinical psychologist. "In the past, if you made a misstep, it was a limited number of people who would know about it."[50] Public embarrassment is especially painful for teens, who are still developing their identities. Social media amplifies the humiliation, putting a vulnerable teen at a higher risk of suicide than teens of the past. John Trautwein, the father of Will Trautwein, a fifteen-year-old in Duluth, Georgia, who took his life in 2010, agrees. "Every single mistake that Will ever made, there was a fear that it would be on YouTube, on Snapchat, on Facebook," remembers John. "They know that if they mess up, everyone will know about it by lunchtime. I did not have to deal with that when I was growing up."[51]

> "If something gets said that's hurtful or humiliating, it's not just the kid who said it who knows, it's the entire school or class."[50]
>
> —Marsha Levy-Warren, clinical psychologist

Mental Health Crisis

Many experts believe that constant exposure to the Internet is fueling teen anxiety, depression, and suicide. "There has been an explosion in numbers in mental health problems amongst youngsters," says Julie Lynn

Evans, a child psychotherapist in Somerset, England. "Something is clearly happening, because I am seeing the evidence in the numbers of depressive, anorexic, cutting children who come to see me. And it always has something to do with the computer, the Internet and the smartphone."[52]

Government health statistics for the United Kingdom and the United States confirm what Evans has seen. In the United Kingdom the National Health Service reports that the number of emergency admissions to child psychiatric wards doubled from 2011 to 2015. According to the US government's Monitoring the Future survey, eighth graders who are heavy users of social media increase their risk of depression by 27 percent, and teens who spend three hours a day or more on electronic devices are 35 percent more likely to have a risk factor for suicide, such as making a suicide plan. "Rates of teen depression and suicide have skyrocketed since 2011,"[53] writes Jean M. Twenge, a psychology professor at San Diego State University and author of the book *iGen: Why Today's Super-connected Kids Are Growing Up Less Rebellious, More Tolerant, Less Happy—and Completely Unprepared for Adulthood*. Twenge uses the word *iGen* to describe the generation of people born from 1995 to 2012. "It's not an exaggeration to describe iGen as being on the brink of the worst mental-health crisis in decades," says Twenge. "Much of this deterioration can be traced to their phones."[54]

> "I am seeing the evidence in the numbers of depressive, anorexic, cutting children who come to see me. And it always has something to do with the computer, the Internet and the smartphone."[52]
>
> —Julie Lynn Evans, child psychotherapist

Twenge believes the pressures of social media are a source of the mental health crisis. "Social media levy a psychic tax on the teen doing the posting, as she anxiously awaits the affirmation of comments and likes," writes Twenge. She cites the example of one of her teenage research subjects, Athena, to support her case. "When Athena posts pictures to Instagram, she told me, 'I'm nervous about what people think and are going to say. It sometimes bugs me when I don't get a certain amount of likes on a picture.'"[55]

Technology Destabilizes Young People

This kind of anxiety is more prevalent among girls than boys, according to Rachel Simmons, author of *Odd Girl Out: The Hidden Culture of Aggression in Girls*. "Social media is girl town," says Simmons. "They are all over it in ways that boys are not." According to Simmons, girls use visual platforms like Instagram, Snapchat, and Facebook more than boys do, and many seek instant approval from their peers, using social media as a measure of their popularity and self-worth. "It used to be that you didn't know how many friends someone had, or what they were doing after school," Simmons says. "Social media assigns numbers to those things. For the most vulnerable girls, that can be very destabilizing."[56]

Twenge believes that destabilization is one reason why depressive symptoms increased 50 percent among girls from 2012 to 2015 but only increased by 21 percent in boys. "The rise in suicide, too, is more pronounced among girls," Twenge points out. "Although the rate increased for both sexes, three times as many 12-to-14-year-old girls killed themselves in 2015 as in 2007, compared with twice as many boys."[57]

The pace of change in technology has outstripped the ability of social institutions to protect the young and vulnerable. Because suicide is an act of self-harm, many people assume that its causes all lie within the individual or the family. But the scientific evidence suggests otherwise. It is time to admit that external factors, including technology, are contributing to the suicide epidemic.

Technology Can Help Prevent Teen Suicide

"[Facebook] Live becomes a lifeline. It opens up the opportunity for people to reach out for support and for people to give support at this time that's critically important."

—Jennifer Guadagno, Facebook's lead researcher for suicide prevention

Quoted in Jessica Guynn, "Facebook Takes Steps to Stop Suicides on Live," *USA Today*, March 1, 2017. www.usatoday.com.

Consider these questions as you read:

1. Do you think it is a good idea to design computer programs that automatically filter out rude or harassing comments on social media sites? Why or why not?
2. Do you think parents should use devices' built-in features to limit the screen time of their teenage children? Why or why not?
3. Would you feel more comfortable discussing an emotional problem face-to-face with a person or anonymously in a group chat? Explain your answer.

Editor's note: The discussion that follows presents common arguments made in support of this perspective, reinforced by facts, quotes, and examples taken from various sources.

There is no doubt that numerous social problems have arisen because of the explosive growth of cell phone, Internet, and social media use. However, technology is getting a bad rap regarding suicide, with some people blaming teens' heavy use of technology for suicidal thoughts and acts. A closer look at the problem reveals technology is not the cause of suicide, however; on the contrary, it can actually serve as a powerful suicide prevention tool. Indeed, suicide is another area in which technology can be used to address the problems it is accused of creating.

Correlation Versus Causation

When researchers announce the findings of a study based on statistics—a study that correlates high levels of screen time with increased suicidal thinking, for example—it is tempting to assume that the one variable causes the other. However, just because two events occur together does not mean that one caused the other. In the case of screen time and suicidal thoughts, it may be that another factor is causing both behaviors. For example, the presence of an abusive parent might cause a teen to spend more time than usual with digital devices as a way to avoid the parent. In addition, it is likely that the abuse is driving the suicidal thinking, not the screen time. Most studies on the matter have thus far revealed correlations but not necessarily causes.

Another problem with blaming technology for teen suicide is that while the number of teens using technology is vast, the number of teen suicides is small. According to Statista, an online business statistics portal, 36 million US teenagers age thirteen to seventeen have access to the Internet, but fewer than 5,000 teens, or 1.5 percent of those with Internet access, take their own lives each year. In fact, the total number of girls age ten to fourteen in the United States who took their lives in 2014 was 150. The loss of even one teen to suicide is devastating to family, friends, and the entire community, but such a small number of cases makes it difficult to identify trends with any degree of confidence.

More Technology, Better Technology

In some cases, such as cyberbullying, the connection between technology and suicide is obvious. The bullying could not take place or would not be as severe without the technology. However, the solution for this is not less technology but more technology and better technology.

For example, technology can be a useful tool in the fight against untraceable apps. Cyberbullies and members of hate groups sometimes hide

Suicide Prevention App Helps One Group of Teens

The iBobbly app was designed to reduce the suicide rate among young Aboriginal Australians, a group with a suicide rate four times higher than the country's national youth average. In a pilot study, sixty-one participants using the iBobbly app (which delivered acceptance-based therapy through various content and activity modules) showed a substantial reduction in PHQ-9 scores that measure depression. Between 50 and 75 percent of all people who die by suicide suffer from depression, so reducing depression can help prevent suicides.

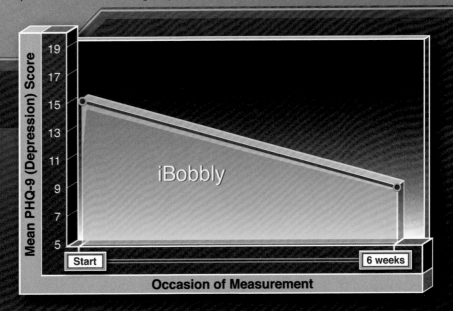

Source: Joseph Tighe et al., "IBobbly Mobile Health Intervention for Suicide Prevention in Australian Indigenous Youth: A Pilot Randomised Controlled Trial," *BMJ Open*, January 27, 2017. http://bmjopen.bmj.com.

behind such apps when harassing people, which makes it difficult for authorities to find and stop them. However, when required by law enforcement or larger technology companies, software developers have changed the technology to make it possible to identify who is using the app to harass others. Technology giants Google and Apple have also helped by making untraceable apps not available in their online stores. For example, in August 2017, Google removed the chat app Gab from its Google

Play store for violating the company's hate speech policy. In a statement, Google said the move was intended to prevent the spread of "content that encourages violence and advocates hate against groups of people."[58]

Most bullying and harassment occurs through more common apps, such as Instagram and Facebook. However, technology is increasingly being used to remove the threat—literally. A recent survey from antibullying charity Ditch the Label found that 42 percent of more than ten thousand British youths age twelve to twenty-five identified Instagram as the platform where they were most bullied—with Facebook next at 37 percent. In June 2017 Instagram announced that it would use a machine-learning algorithm known as DeepText to filter certain offensive comments and block them. If a user posts offensive or harassing language, DeepText will catch it and delete it instantly. "Machine learning algorithms have proven to be effective ways to detect hate speech and cyberbullying,"[59] says Tom Davidson, coauthor of reports on hate speech and cyberbullying on social media.

> "Machine learning algorithms have proven to be effective ways to detect hate speech and cyberbullying."[59]
>
> —Tom Davidson, cyberbullying researcher

Internet-Based Suicide Prevention

Technology can also help prevent suicide when companies offer tools and platforms that are specifically designed to help those at risk. For example, in March 2017 Facebook announced it would integrate suicide prevention tools into Facebook Live, the video chat app that some people have used to live-stream their suicides. "There have been terribly tragic events—like suicides, some live streamed—that perhaps could have been prevented if someone had realized what was happening and reported them sooner," wrote Facebook cofounder Mark Zuckerberg. Zuckerberg was no doubt referring to a tragedy that occurred in January 2017, when a fourteen-year-old girl hung herself in her Florida foster home on Facebook Live, and to a young Turkish man who in October 2016 took his life in front of the camera after breaking up with his girlfriend. Facebook

Live's suicide prevention tool will allow users concerned about someone who is streaming about suicide to reach out to the person and also report the video to Facebook. Facebook will automatically display suicide prevention resources on the screen of the at-risk person and provide resources for the person who reported the stream.

Facebook is also testing an artificial intelligence program, similar to the one used to prevent bullying at Instagram (which Facebook owns), to identify warning signs of suicide in Facebook posts and comments. The goal is to use the advanced technology to identify at-risk people in real time and connect them with those who can help. "One of the things we have learned from experts is that social support is one of the best ways to prevent suicide,"[60] says Jennifer Guadagno, Facebook's lead researcher for suicide prevention.

Suicide Prevention Apps Can Help

In a similar vein, suicide prevention professionals are trying to use cell phone apps to identify at-risk teens and stop them from taking their lives. Dozens of mental health and suicide prevention apps are now available, including Stay Alive, LifeLine, R U Suicidal?, DMHS Suicide Prevention App, and Operation Life. Most of the apps provide a list of warning signs that the user can check to see if he or she is at risk. The DMHS Suicide Prevention App includes an interactive self-test featuring a chatbot (chosen by the user), who asks various questions as if chatting via text. Depending on the user's replies, the chatbot will suggest steps for the user to take. Most apps also let the user create a safety plan to follow if they are feeling suicidal. Some include pictures of loved ones the user has chosen that encourage the user to stay alive.

> "One of the things we have learned from experts is that social support is one of the best ways to prevent suicide."[60]
>
> —Jennifer Guadagno, Facebook's lead researcher for suicide prevention

One of the strengths of cell phone apps is that they let the user seek help without having to discuss intimate details of their lives with other people. Teens are often reluctant to discuss suicide or mental health problems because they find it embarrassing. The apps can help a teen discuss difficult issues without fearing he or she will be identified by family or friends. Anonymity also helps some people feel more willing to say things they otherwise would keep private. "The ability to remain anonymous in a conversational community increases the willingness to confess and discuss thoughts and feelings related to suicide, mental pain and vulnerability, while reducing the risk of self-censorship,"[61] write researchers at Karolinska Institute in Solna, Sweden.

Technology also offers a way for at-risk teens located in remote areas to receive help and treatment that is otherwise unavailable. Mental health professionals increasingly use online chat, video, and e-mail platforms to consult with those at risk of suicide. A study conducted in Japan and published in *Crisis: The Journal of Crisis Intervention and Suicide Prevention* in January 2017 found that such consultations can be effective. The researchers placed online ads to identify people at risk for suicide and offered them e-mail consultations to assess their suicide risk, provide them with support, and help them locate behavioral health services. A total of 139 people responded to the ads and used the service, which consisted of supportive listening, risk assessment, and offering advice for how or where to seek additional help. The researchers found that suicidal thoughts were present in 74 percent of the subjects, and 12 percent had a history of suicide attempts. After consultation, 10.8 percent of the subjects reported a positive change in mood. Sixteen percent of the users showed intentions to seek help from new supporters, and 10 percent took help-seeking actions.

The same technological methods that have led to breakthroughs in other areas of computing, such as machine learning and artificial intelligence, are now being applied to mental health and suicide prevention. A period of testing is required to find out which techniques and apps are most effective, but technology is already being used to save lives, and there is little doubt that it will make a large contribution to suicide prevention in the future.

Chapter Four

Are Suicide Prevention Programs Effective?

Teen Suicide Prevention Programs Are Not Working

- The United States is moving away from its goal of achieving lower suicide rates.
- Despite decades of prevention efforts, professionals have not gotten any better at assessing who is at risk for suicide.
- It is not possible to prevent the large percentage of impulsive suicides.

The Debate at a Glance

Teen Suicide Prevention Programs Are Working

- Research has shown that some suicide prevention programs can reduce suicide rates.
- Psychotherapy has been shown to be effective at preventing suicide among people who have already engaged in self-harm.
- The problem is not the suicide prevention techniques but rather finding a way to provide them to the people most at risk.

Teen Suicide Prevention Programs Are Not Working

"We may well be putting our own professional anxieties above the needs of service users and, paradoxically, increasing the risks of suicide."

—Melissa K.Y. Chan and colleagues, public health researchers

Quoted in Declan Murray and Patrick Devitt, "Suicide Risk Assessment Doesn't Work," *Scientific American*, March 28, 2017. www.scientificamerican.com.

Consider these questions as you read:

1. Does the increasing rate of suicides prove that suicide prevention programs are not effective? Why or why not?
2. Do you think mental health professionals should spend less time using screening tests? Explain your answer.
3. Do you believe some people take their lives without warning, or do other people just miss the signs? Explain your answer.

Editor's note: The discussion that follows presents common arguments made in support of this perspective, reinforced by facts, quotes, and examples taken from various sources.

The news from the CDC was grim: The United States is not only failing to meet the agency's targets for reducing teen suicide, but it is moving in the wrong direction. In 2010 the CDC set out to improve public health in twenty-six areas by 2020—an initiative called Healthy People 2020. By its midcourse review released in January 2017, however, the CDC reported that suicide rates among teens are going up, not down, and moving away from the 2020 targets. Yet at the same time, young people are receiving more medical attention for mental health problems than ever before. This combination of increased suicide rates amid widespread suicide prevention can mean only one thing—mental health treatments are on the rise, but they are not reducing suicide.

Suicide Risk Assessment Has Failed

Preventing suicide begins with accurately identifying who is most at risk, but current methods of risk assessment have failed. A scientific study conducted in 2016 by researchers in Australia found that suicide risk assessment had not become any more accurate over the past forty years. The researchers found that just as many suicides occurred among patients identified as low risk as among those identified as high risk. In other words, the assessments were not accurately predicting who would actually take their own lives. "Despite decades of research . . . suicide risk categorization remains uncertain," write the researchers. "The extent of this uncertainty is profound and our results are not reassuring. It remains to be seen if methods can be developed to consistently and clearly distinguish high-risk from lower-risk patients."[62]

Roger Mulder, a psychiatrist at the University of Otago in Dunedin, New Zealand, agrees with the Australian group's findings. He has found that 60 percent of the people he studied who took their own lives had been categorized as low risk. "We've had a 20- or 30-year experiment which hasn't worked,"[63] Mulder says.

A 2016 study by researchers in the United Kingdom also found failures in suicide risk assessment. In their study, the researchers focused on people who had already harmed themselves, usually by attempting suicide. They found that the four greatest risk factors—previous episodes of self-harm, suicidal intent, physical health problems, and being male—were so common that they did not help identify who was most at risk. Without clear markers of who is at risk, treatment cannot be targeted to the right people. If the right people are not treated, suicide prevention will fail.

The Tools and Tests Do Not Work

Part of the problem with identifying who is at risk is that the tests and tools that most professionals rely on do not seem to work. The British researchers looked at the most common methods of interpreting

Students Do Not Take Advantage of Prevention Programs

Although many US colleges have increased their suicide prevention programs, many students (both teens and young adults) are not taking advantage of them. BestColleges.com reports that although 44 percent of college students have symptoms of depression, 75 percent of college students do not seek help for their mental health problems. The likely reason is the ongoing stigma associated with depression and other mental health issues. This is one reason why suicide prevention is not working.

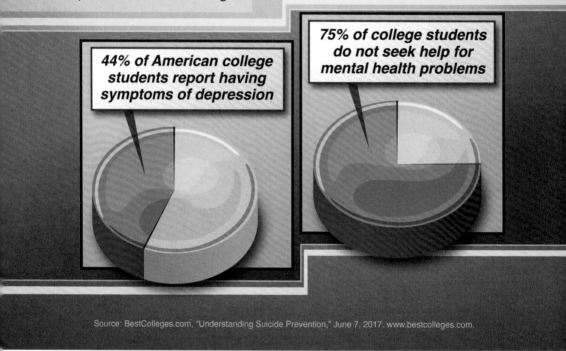

44% of American college students report having symptoms of depression

75% of college students do not seek help for mental health problems

Source: BestColleges.com, "Understanding Suicide Prevention," June 7, 2017. www.bestcolleges.com.

the answers patients give health care professionals about their feelings of anxiety, sadness, and hopelessness. The tools used for evaluating the patients' answers, known as scales, did not detect the patients most at risk. In fact, such tools might do more harm than good, the researchers say, because the professionals are misled by the results and lulled into a sense of complacency that they are helping those who most need it. "The use of these scales, or an over-reliance on the identification of risk factors in clinical practice, may provide false reassurance and is, therefore, potentially dangerous,"[64] write the researchers. Relying too much on risk-assessment tools can lead mental health professionals to overlook other possible warning signs of suicide.

As a result of faulty risk assessment, many teens are hospitalized who are not really a danger to themselves. Mental health professionals may order hospitalization out of a fear of being blamed if they do not intervene in some way. According to Mulder, suicidal patients often are hospitalized "to reduce staff anxiety rather than for their treatment needs." Indeed, increased hospitalization has not reduced the suicide rate. It is therefore time to look at new tools and techniques for suicide prevention. "New approaches are required," says Mulder, "possibly public health, sociological, community or combinations in addition to, or instead of, medical approaches."[65]

> "An over-reliance on the identification of risk factors in clinical practice, may provide false reassurance and is, therefore, potentially dangerous."[64]
>
> —Melissa K.Y. Chan and colleagues, public health researchers

No Warning

One of the reasons that risk assessment often fails is that people who are determined to take their own lives do not give truthful answers when questioned by doctors and other mental health professionals. They know that if they tell the truth about their suicidal thoughts, people will try to stop them from carrying out their plans. "The paradox is that the people who are most intent on committing suicide know that they have to keep their plans to themselves if they are to carry out the act," says Michael Miller, assistant professor of psychiatry at Harvard Medical School. "Thus, the people most in need of help may be the toughest to save."[66] Secrecy is one of the biggest factors working against suicide prevention efforts.

On the other hand, some people do not plan their suicides at all, and this also causes suicide prevention to fail. According to Annmarie Dadoly, former editor of Harvard Health, from 30 percent to 80 percent of suicides are impulsive, with just minutes or an hour elapsing between the time a person decides on suicide and when he or she commits the act. Such suicides are nearly impossible to stop. "When individuals suddenly take their own lives with no warning, all we can do is look to each other for support," says Patrick J. Skerrett, former executive editor of Harvard Health. "It may be natural to ask, 'What did I miss?' But we should remind ourselves what experts say: This kind of death defies prediction."[67] Because of suicide's unpredictable and secret nature, prevention programs will always have a limit regarding what they can achieve.

Another problem with suicide prevention programs is that they are not integrated with other mental health programs. "We have more and more effective treatments, but we have to figure out how to bake them into health care systems so they are used more automatically," says Dr. Jane Pearson, chair of the NIMH's Suicide Research Consortium. "We've got bits and pieces, but we haven't really put them all together yet."[68] For example, mental health professionals are often highly skilled at treating disorders such as anxiety and depression, but because suicidal behavior is rarer, they are not as knowledgeable about how to handle it.

> "The people who are most intent on committing suicide know that they have to keep their plans to themselves if they are to carry out the act. Thus, the people most in need of help may be the toughest to save."[66]
>
> —Michael Miller, assistant professor of psychiatry at Harvard Medical School

To close this knowledge gap, in 2017 California passed a law requiring psychologists to undergo suicide prevention training when they get or renew their clinical license. When it goes into effect in 2020, the bill, known as AB89, will require professionals to complete a minimum of six hours of course work or fieldwork in suicide risk assessment and intervention. In doing so, California joins eight other states (Indiana, Kentucky, Nevada, New Hampshire, Pennsylvania, Tennessee, Utah, and Washington) in mandating training in suicide assessment, treatment, and management for health professionals. This is a step in the right direction, but more must be done to make suicide prevention effective.

Teen Suicide Prevention Programs Are Working

"A global review of suicide prevention strategies . . . concluded that combinations of evidence based approaches do work."

—Mark Rowland, director of communications for the Mental Health Foundation

Mark Rowland, "Preventing Suicide: Supporting Those Who Don't Reach Out Directly for Help," Mental Health Foundation, September 8, 2017. www.mentalhealth.org.uk.

Consider these questions as you read:

1. Do you think enough is being done to identify who is at risk of suicide? Why or why not?
2. Have you ever asked anyone if he or she had thoughts about committing suicide? If so, what did the person say? If not, do you think you could bring up the subject if someone seemed troubled?
3. Would you feel comfortable recommending a campus counseling program to a friend? Why or why not?

Editor's note: The discussion that follows presents common arguments made in support of this perspective, reinforced by facts, quotes, and examples taken from various sources.

There is no denying that teen suicide rates are climbing. The latest data from the CDC shows that suicide rates for US middle school students have surpassed the rate of death by car crashes for the first time since the CDC started keeping suicide statistics. These numbers suggest to some that suicide prevention strategies are failing, but this is the wrong conclusion to draw from the data. It is entirely possible and even likely that the number of suicides would have been even higher *without* suicide prevention programs in place. It is a grim and sad fact that it is easier to count suicides than it is to count lives that have been saved by suicide prevention. A rising suicide rate in and of itself proves nothing. Suicide prevention programs must be evaluated on their own—and when they are, they are shown to be effective.

Approaches That Work

It is worth noting that the United States does not lead the world in suicides; far from it. The United States ranks forty-eighth in the world for suicides per 100,000 people, according to WHO's 2015 statistics. The United States has 12.6 suicides per 100,000, while South Korea has almost double the number (24.1), and Sri Lanka almost three times as many (34.6). America's suicide prevention programs are likely one reason why its suicide rate is as low as it is. The fact is that most if not all of the countries with the highest rates of suicide—such as Guyana, Mongolia, and Kazakhstan—do not have highly developed suicide prevention programs, if any at all.

Researchers who have studied suicide prevention programs have found that they work. For example, a team of researchers led by Natalie B.V. Riblet of Dartmouth College reviewed seventy-eight patient trials to determine just how effective suicide prevention strategies are. Each trial compared patients who received suicide prevention care to ones who did not (known as a control group). The researchers found that a WHO suicide prevention program known as BIC (brief intervention and contact) was associated with significantly lower odds of suicide. "The WHO BIC program is a promising suicide prevention strategy,"[69] concluded the researchers.

> "The WHO BIC [brief intervention and contact] program is a promising suicide prevention strategy."[69]
>
> —Natalie B.V. Riblet and colleagues, public health researchers

Other researchers have found that a specific mental health treatment known as psychotherapy can prevent suicide. A team of researchers led by Annette Erlangsen, an associate professor at the Johns Hopkins Bloomberg School of Public Health, looked at the health records of 5,678 Danes who had engaged in self-harm and then received eight to ten weeks of

School-Based Suicide Prevention Program Lowers Suicide Attempts

Teens who took part in a school-based suicide prevention program had fewer suicide attempts than teens who did not go through the program. This was the finding of Swedish researchers who studied the effects of the Youth Aware of Mental Health (YAM) suicide prevention program. Their subjects, age fourteen to sixteen, included students from 168 public schools in ten European countries. Students were evaluated at three-month and twelve-month intervals. After three months, researchers noted, nineteen YAM participants reported suicide attempts compared with twenty-seven in a control group (students who did not take part in a suicide prevention program). At twelve months, the difference was even greater: Fourteen YAM participants had attempted suicide compared to thirty-four in the control group.

	3-Month Follow-Up		12-Month Follow-Up	
	Number of Study Participants	Number of Suicide Attempts	Number of Study Participants	Number of Suicide Attempts
YAM Participants	2,166	19	1,987	14
Control Group	2,366	27	2,256	34

Note: The number of participants varies at the 3-month and 12-month follow-ups for various reasons, including school absences unrelated to the study.

Source: Danuta Wasserman et al., "School-Based Suicide Prevention Programmes: The SEYLE Cluster-Randomised, Controlled Trial," Lancet, April 18, 2015. https://cps.memberclicks.net.

psychosocial therapy at suicide prevention clinics. The researchers compared these subjects with 17,034 people who had engaged in self-harm but received standard care, including admission to a hospital, referral for treatment, or discharge with no referral. The researchers matched the groups by more than thirty characteristics to ensure that any differences they found were the result of the suicide prevention care and not due to genetics, overall health, behavior, or economic standing. Over a twenty-year period, 16.5 percent of the treated group repeated the act of self-harm, compared with 19.1 percent of the untreated group. In the treated group,

1.6 percent died by suicide, compared with 2.2 percent of the untreated. Put a different way, the researchers concluded that 153 deaths, including 30 deaths by suicide, were prevented by the suicide prevention treatments. "Suicide is a rare event," said Erlangsen, "and you need a huge sample to study it. We had that, and we were able to find a significant effect."[70]

Identifying Those Most at Risk

The real problem with suicide prevention programs is not that the techniques do not work, but rather that they are not being provided to the patients who need them most. A massive study published in July 2017 found that more attention needs to be paid to patients who are discharged from hospitals after being admitted with suicidal thoughts. According to the study, the suicide rate for the discharged patients was 484 per 100,000 people, or about thirty-eight times greater than the overall US rate of 12.6 per 100,000. The suicide rate within three months after discharge was an astronomical 1,132 per 100,000 people. The rate dropped to 494 for studies with follow-up periods of one to five years, 366 for studies with follow-up periods of five to ten years, and 277 for studies with follow-up periods longer than ten years. But the ten-year period is still twenty times higher than the US national suicide rate.

Clearly, recently discharged psychiatric patients are at the greatest risk of suicide, but many are not receiving any suicide prevention care. According to a 2016 study by Mark Olfson of Columbia University, only about half of US psychiatric patients receive any outpatient care during the first week after hospital discharge, and one-third receive no mental health care during the first month. These studies suggest that it is not that suicide prevention strategies do not work; rather, they are not being provided to the people who need them most—namely, patients being discharged from hospitals after suicidal episodes.

Encouraging People to Seek Help

Suicide prevention efforts can only work when people at risk seek help, and researchers are learning surprising things about the kinds of campaigns that make them more likely to do that. Consider what happened when five different US colleges and universities launched a campaign to encourage students at risk for suicide to use campus counseling centers.

The campaign used both student and celebrity spokespeople to encourage students to seek professional mental health help as a suicide prevention strategy. Compared to students in the control group (who were not exposed to any campaign messages), students who received the campaign messages were more likely to refer a friend to the university counseling center and more likely to visit the counseling center for a mental health concern. In addition, it turned out that the campaigns that featured students were more effective than the ones that featured celebrities. Students living in areas that received messages featuring their peers reported a greater willingness to refer friends to the counseling center, compared to those who lived in areas that received celebrity messages and those who lived in areas that received no messages. "Results of this study . . . support the need for continued exposure to campaign messages to impact health outcomes,"[71] conclude the researchers.

> "Acknowledging and talking about suicide may in fact reduce rather than increase suicidal thoughts."[73]
>
> —The NIMH

Talking about suicide at the high school and middle school levels is another suicide prevention strategy that has met with success. "Kids spend a lot of time at school . . . it's where they live their lives,"[72] says David Jobes, who heads the Suicide Prevention Lab at Catholic University in Washington, DC. Many educators do not feel comfortable talking about suicide, mainly because they are not sure what to say. Many are afraid that if they bring up suicide, students will start to think about it. However, research suggests this is not the case. "Studies show that asking at-risk individuals if they are suicidal does not increase suicides or suicidal thoughts," says the NIMH. "Acknowledging and talking about suicide may in fact reduce rather than increase suicidal thoughts." Getting a student to talk about his or her suicidal feelings is crucial, according to the NIMH, which puts "Ask: 'Are you thinking about killing yourself?'" as the very first step on its "5 Action Steps for Helping Someone in Emotional Pain." The NIMH advice applies not only to educators, but also to family members and friends at school. When the person answers a question about suicide, the NIMH advises to "listen carefully and learn what the individual is thinking and feeling."[73] If it seems like the person is at risk, a family member, friend, spiritual adviser, or mental health professional should be notified.

The recent rise in teen suicide in the United States is an alarming trend, but it is a mistake to think that it means suicide prevention efforts do not work. Studies show that when prevention programs are used, suicide rates can be reduced. What is needed is more programs, more people freely talking about them, and better targeting of the resources. "Suicide is preventable,"[74] says the CDC. This is not just a slogan. It is a medical fact.

Source Notes

Overview: A Deadly Epidemic

1. Quoted in Sabrina Tavernise, "U.S. Suicide Rate Surges to a 30-Year High," *New York Times*, April 22, 2016. www.nytimes.com.
2. Quoted in Peter Stanford, "Are Smartphones Making Our Children Mentally Ill?," *Telegraph* (London), March 21, 2015. www.telegraph.co.uk.
3. Deb Stone et al., *Preventing Suicide: A Technical Package of Policy, Programs, and Practices*. Atlanta: National Center for Injury Prevention and Control, Centers for Disease Control and Prevention, 2017, p. 7.
4. Office of the Surgeon General and National Action Alliance for Suicide Prevention, "2012 National Strategy for Suicide Prevention: Goals and Objectives for Action," 2012. www.surgeongeneral.gov.
5. Quoted in Office of the Surgeon General and National Action Alliance for Suicide Prevention, "2012 National Strategy for Suicide Prevention."
6. Stone et al., *Preventing Suicide*, p. 8.
7. Mayo Clinic Staff, "Risk Factors," Mayo Clinic, August 28, 2015. www.mayoclinic.org.
8. Quoted in World Health Organization, "Suicide Huge but Preventable Public Health Problem," September 8, 2004. www.who.int.

Chapter One: Do Antidepressant Drugs Contribute to the Problem of Teen Suicide?

9. Quoted in Brian, "Reece, Aged 17," AntiDepAware, May 13, 2016. http://antidepaware.co.uk.
10. Quoted in Brian, "Reece, Aged 17."
11. Quoted in Brian, "Reece, Aged 17."
12. Quoted in Robert T. Muller, "Antidepressants and Teen Suicide," *Talking About Trauma* (blog), *Psychology Today*, May 31, 2013. www.psychologytoday.com.

13. National Institute of Mental Health, "Antidepressant Medications for Children and Adolescents: Information for Parents and Caregivers," National Institutes of Health. www.nimh.nih.gov.

14. Quoted in Caroline Scott, "Can Pills for Depression Turn You into a Killer? In a Shocking Interview, a Man Who Calls Himself a Loving Father Tells How He Killed His Son During a Psychotic Episode, Caused, He Says, by Medication," *Daily Mail* (London), July 24, 2017. www.dailymail.co.uk.

15. Joanna Moncrieff, "Misrepresenting Harms in Antidepressant Trials," *BMJ*, January 28, 2016. www.bmj.com.

16. Tarang Sharma et al., "Suicidality and Aggression During Antidepressant Treatment: Systematic Review and Meta-analyses Based on Clinical Study Reports," *BMJ*, January 27, 2016. www.bmj.com.

17. Quoted in Sarah Knapton, "Antidepressants Can Raise the Risk of Suicide, Biggest Ever Review Finds," *Telegraph* (London), January 27, 2016. www.telegraph.co.uk.

18. Tracy, "Stolen Lives," Pill That Steals Lives. www.thepillthatsteals.com.

19. Gardiner Harris, "F.D.A. Links Drugs to Being Suicidal," *New York Times*, September 14, 2004. www.nytimes.com.

20. Quoted in Christine Y. Lu et al., "Changes in Antidepressant Use by Young People and Suicidal Behavior After FDA Warnings and Media Coverage: Quasi-experimental Study," *BMJ*, June 18, 2014. www.bmj.com.

21. Quoted in Susan Donaldson James, "Doctors Call: End Warning on Antidepressants or Risk Suicides," ABC News, July 9, 2014. http://abcnews.go.com.

22. Howard LeWine, "Teen Suicide Tries Increased After FDA Toughened Antidepressant Warning," *Harvard Health Blog*, June 20, 2014. www.health.harvard.edu.

23. Quoted in Rob Stein, "Warnings Against Antidepressants for Teens May Have Backfired," NPR, June 18, 2014. www.npr.org.

24. Lu et al., "Changes in Antidepressant Use by Young People and Suicidal Behavior After FDA Warnings and Media Coverage."

25. Quoted in James, "Doctors Call."

26. Robert D. Gibbons et al., "Early Evidence on the Effects of Regulators' Suicidality Warnings on SSRI Prescriptions and Suicide in

Children and Adolescents," *American Journal of Psychiatry*, September 1, 2007, p. 1356.

27. Jeffrey A. Bridge et al., "Clinical Response and Risk for Reported Suicidal Ideation and Suicide Attempts in Pediatric Antidepressant Treatment: A Meta-analysis of Randomized Controlled Trials," *Journal of the American Medical Association*, April 18, 2007. www.ncbi .nlm.nih.gov.

28. Mayo Clinic Staff, "Antidepressants for Children and Teens," Mayo Clinic, May 27, 2016. www.mayoclinic.org.

29. Harold S. Koplewicz, "Antidepressants and Teen Suicides," Child Mind Institute, January 9, 2017. https://childmind.org.

Chapter Two: Is the Media Contributing to the Rise in Teen Suicide?

30. Quoted in Catherine Saint Louis, "For Families of Teens at Suicide Risk, '13 Reasons' Raises Concerns," *New York Times*, May 1, 2017. www.nytimes.com.

31. John W. Ayers et al., "Internet Searches for Suicide Following the Release of *13 Reasons Why*," *JAMA Internal Medicine*, July 31, 2017. http://jamanetwork.com.

32. Quoted in Madhumita Murgia, "Internet Searches on Suicide Went Up After '13 Reasons Why' Released by Netflix," *Washington Post*, July 31, 2017. www.washingtonpost.com.

33. Quoted in Murgia, "Internet Searches on Suicide Went Up After '13 Reasons Why' Released by Netflix."

34. Quoted in Fox News, "Families Blame '13 Reasons Why' for 2 Teens' Suicides," June 27, 2017. www.foxnews.com.

35. Quoted in Stephen J. Dubner, "The Suicide Paradox: Full Transcript," Freakonomics (podcast), August 31, 2011. http://freakonomics.com.

36. Quoted in Dubner, "The Suicide Paradox."

37. Quoted in Joyce Chen, "Selena Gomez Defends '13 Reasons Why' as Honest Depiction of Teen Suicide," *Rolling Stone*, June 7, 2017. http://www.rollingstone.com.

38. Nic Sheff, "*13 Reasons Why* Writer: Why We Didn't Shy Away from Hannah's Suicide," *Vanity Fair*, April 19, 2017. www.vanityfair.com.

39. Ayers et al., "Internet Searches for Suicide Following the Release of *13 Reasons Why*."

40. Quoted in Murgia, "Internet Searches on Suicide Went Up After '13 Reasons Why' Released by Netflix."

41. Ayers et al., "Internet Searches for Suicide Following the Release of *13 Reasons Why*."

42. Quoted in Jacqueline Howard, "Why Teen Mental Health Experts Are Focused on '13 Reasons Why,'" CNN, April 25, 2017. http://edition.cnn.com.

43. Quoted in Saint Louis, "For Families of Teens at Suicide Risk, '13 Reasons' Raises Concerns."

44. Quoted in Saint Louis, "For Families of Teens at Suicide Risk, '13 Reasons' Raises Concerns."

45. Quoted in Keerthi Mohan, "Robin Williams Suicide: The Academy Under Attack for 'Genie, You're Free' Tweet," *International Business Times*, August 14, 2014. http://www.ibtimes.co.in.

46. William Proctor, "Open Letter to Journalists, Mental Health Campaigners and Psychologists," Bournemouth University, May 25, 2017. www1.bournemouth.ac.uk.

Chapter Three: Do New Technologies Contribute to Teen Suicide?

47. Quoted in Lucy Pasha-Robinson, "Teenager Killed Herself in Front of Parents After 'Relentless' Cyber Bullying," *Independent* (London), December 2, 2016. www.independent.co.uk.

48. Quoted in Caitlin Keating, "Teen's Family Reveals the Intense Bullying Before Her Suicide in Front of Them: 'It Was Stalking,'" *People*, December 14, 2016. http://people.com.

49. Quoted in Keating, "Teen's Family Reveals the Intense Bullying Before Her Suicide in Front of Them."

50. Quoted in Sabrina Tavernise, "Young Adolescents as Likely to Die from Suicide as from Traffic Accidents," *New York Times*, November 3, 2016. www.nytimes.com.

51. Quoted in Sonya Collins, "Teen Suicide: 'The Time for Secrecy Is Over,'" WebMD, July 25, 2017. www.webmd.com.

52. Quoted in Stanford, "Are Smartphones Making Our Children Mentally Ill?"

53. Jean M. Twenge, "Have Smartphones Destroyed a Generation?," *Atlantic*, September 2017. www.theatlantic.com.

54. Twenge, "Have Smartphones Destroyed a Generation?"

55. Twenge, "Have Smartphones Destroyed a Generation?"

56. Quoted in Tavernise, "Young Adolescents as Likely to Die from Suicide as from Traffic Accidents."

57. Twenge, "Have Smartphones Destroyed a Generation?"

58. Quoted in Amar Toor, "Google Removes Gab App for Violating Hate Speech Policy," Verge, August 18, 2017. www.theverge.com.

59. Quoted in Macy Bayern, "How AI Became Instagram's Weapon of Choice in the War on Cyberbullying," *TechRepublic*, August 14, 2017. www.techrepublic.com.

60. Quoted in Jessica Guynn, "Facebook Takes Steps to Stop Suicides on Live," *USA Today*, March 1, 2017. www.usatoday.com.

61. Tony Durkee et al., "Internet Pathways in Suicidality: A Review of the Evidence," ResearchGate, October 2011. www.researchgate.net.

Chapter Four: Are Suicide Prevention Programs Effective?

62. Matthew Large et al., "Meta-analysis of Longitudinal Cohort Studies of Suicide Risk Assessment Among Psychiatric Patients: Heterogeneity in Results and Lack of Improvement over Time," *PLOS ONE*, June 10, 2016. http://journals.plos.org.

63. Quoted in Simon Collins, "Hairdressers Learn to Help the Suicidal," *New Zealand Herald* (Auckland), September 11, 2013. www.nzherald.co.nz.

64. Melissa K.Y. Chan et al., "Predicting Suicide Following Self-Harm: Systematic Review of Risk Factors and Risk Scales," *British Journal of Psychiatry*, October 2016. http://bjp.rcpsych.org.

65. Quoted in Maria Bradshaw, "Psychiatry & Suicide Prevention: A 30-Year Failed Experiment," Mad in America, September 17, 2013. www.madinamerica.com.

66. Quoted in Patrick J. Skerrett, "Suicide Often Not Preceded by Warnings," *Harvard Health Blog*, October 29, 2015. www.health.harvard.edu.

67. Skerrett, "Suicide Often Not Preceded by Warnings."

68. Quoted in Tavernise, "U.S. Suicide Rate Surges to a 30-Year High."

69. Natalie B.V. Riblet et al., "Strategies to Prevent Death by Suicide: Meta-analysis of Randomised Controlled Trials," *British Journal of Psychiatry*, June 2017. www.ncbi.nlm.nih.gov.

70. Quoted in Nicholas Bakalar, "Therapy Prevents Repeat Suicide Attempts," *Well* (blog), *New York Times*, December 1, 2014. https://well.blogs.nytimes.com.

71. Kami J. Silk et al., "Evaluation of a Social Norms Approach to a Suicide Prevention Campaign," *Journal of Health Communications*, January 18, 2017. www.ncbi.nlm.nih.gov.

72. Quoted in Elissa Nadworny, "Middle School Suicides Reach an All-Time High," NPR, November 4, 2016. www.npr.org.

73. National Institute of Mental Health, "Suicide Prevention," March 2017. www.nimh.nih.gov.

74. Centers for Disease Control and Prevention, "Preventing Suicide: A Comprehensive Public Health Approach," September 15, 2015. www.cdc.gov.

Teen Suicide Facts

Suicide Globally

- According to WHO, approximately eight hundred thousand people die by suicide annually.
- WHO reports that for each suicide, six to eight other people are profoundly affected by a devastating grief.
- A WHO report found that the global suicide rate is 11.4 per 100,000 people; 15.0 per 100,000 for males and 8.0 per 100,000 for females.
- Globally, suicide is the second-leading cause of death in fifteen- to twenty-nine-year-olds, according to WHO.

Suicide Among Teens

- Four out of five teens who attempt suicide have given clear warning signs, according to the NIMH.
- According to the CDC, annually, one in five teenagers in the United States seriously considers suicide.
- According to the CDC, suicide is the second leading cause of death for youth ages ten to twenty-four.
- According to the CDC, suicide is the second leading cause of death for college-age youth and those ages twelve to eighteen.
- The CDC reports that more teenagers and young adults die from suicide than from cancer, heart disease, AIDS, birth defects, stroke, pneumonia, influenza, and chronic lung disease combined.
- Each day, there are an average of over 3,470 suicide attempts by young people in grades nine to twelve, according to the CDC.
- The CDC reports that suicide claims an average of more than one hundred young lives each week.

Suicide by Gender, Race, and Ethnicity

- According to the CDC, females attempt suicide more than three times as often as males.
- The CDC reports that males die by suicide more than four times as often as females.
- Among those ages ten to twenty-four, 81 percent of the suicide deaths were males and 19 percent were females, reports the CDC.
- According to the CDC, Native American/Alaskan Native youth have the highest rates of suicide.
- The CDC reports that Caucasian youth have the second-highest rate of suicide.
- According to the CDC, African American youth have the third-highest rate of suicide.
- Hispanic youth are more likely to report having attempted suicide than their black or white non-Hispanic peers, according to the CDC.

Lesbian, Gay, Bisexual, Transgender, and Questioning Suicide Risk Factors

- Lesbian, gay, bisexual, transgender, and questioning (LGBTQ) youth are at higher risk for suicide than their heterosexual peers, according to the NIMH.
- According to the National School Climate Survey (NSCS), 81.9 percent of LGBT students have experienced harassment at school because of their sexual orientation.
- According to the NSCS, 63.5 percent of LGBT students have felt unsafe at school.
- According to the NSCS, 60.4 percent of LGBT students never reported an incident of harassment or bullying to school personnel.

Related Organizations and Websites

Alliance of Hope for Suicide Loss Survivors

website: www.allianceofhope.org

Alliance for Hope for Suicide Loss Survivors is a nonprofit organization that provides information to help survivors understand the complex emotional aftermath of suicide. The website features a blog, bookstore, and memorials.

American Association of Suicidology (AAS)

5221 Wisconsin Ave. NW

Washington, DC 20015

e-mail: www.suicidology.org/about-aas/contact-us

website: www.suicidology.org

Founded in 1968 by Edwin S. Shneidman, the AAS promotes research, public awareness programs, public education, and training for professionals and volunteers. In addition, the AAS serves as a national clearinghouse for information on suicide. Its mission is to promote the understanding and prevention of suicide and support those who have been affected by it.

American Foundation for Suicide Prevention (AFSP)

120 Wall St., 29th Floor

New York, NY 10005

e-mail: info@afsp.org

website: www.afsp.org

Established in 1987, the AFSP is a voluntary health organization. The foundation is dedicated to saving lives and bringing hope to those affected by suicide. It offers those affected by suicide a nationwide community and supports them through education, advocacy, and research.

AntiDepAware

e-mail: brian@antidepaware.co.uk

website: www.antidepaware.co.uk

Founded by the father of a man who took his life shortly after being prescribed the antidepressant citalopram, AntiDepAware is designed to promote awareness of the dangers of antidepressants. It includes links to reports of suicide inquests held in England and Wales since 2003, as well as profiles of dozens of young people who took their own lives.

Centre for Suicide Prevention

105 Twelfth Ave. SE, Suite 320

Calgary, AB, Canada T2G 1A1

website: www.siec.ca

Established in 1981, the Centre for Suicide Prevention is a nonprofit organization that is a branch of the Canadian Mental Health Association. Its mission is to educate people with the information, knowledge, and skills necessary to respond to people at risk of suicide.

Jason Foundation

18 Volunteer Dr.

Hendersonville, TN 37075

e-mail: contact@jasonfoundation.com

website: www.jasonfoundation.com

The Jason Foundation is a US organization that provides curriculum material to schools, parents, and other teens about how teen suicide can be preventable. It is dedicated to the prevention of the silent epidemic of youth suicide through educational and awareness programs that equip young people, educators, youth workers, and parents with the tools and resources to help identify and assist at-risk youth.

Sibling Survivors of Suicide Loss

website: www.siblingsurvivors.com

The Sibling Survivors of Suicide Loss site aims to provide a safe place for anyone who has lost a sister or brother to suicide. It is a place for people who have lost a sibling to suicide to share memories, discuss their feelings and experiences, and to share photos. It is also a place to connect with others who have lost a sister or brother to suicide.

Trevor Project

PO Box 69232
West Hollywood, CA 90069
e-mail: info@thetrevorproject.org
website: www.thetrevorproject.org

Founded in 1998 by the creators of the Academy Award–winning short film *Trevor*, the Trevor Project is a national organization providing crisis intervention and suicide prevention services to LGBTQ young people ages thirteen to twenty-four.

For Further Research

Books

Amy Bleuel, *Project Semicolon: Your Story Isn't Over*. New York: Harper-Collins, 2017.

Cherese Cartlidge, *Teens and Suicide*. San Diego, CA: ReferencePoint, 2017.

Connie Goldsmith, *Understanding Suicide: A National Epidemic*. Minneapolis, MN: Twenty-First Century, 2016.

Keith Jones, *Suicide Information for Teens*. Detroit, MI: Omnigraphics, 2017.

Jean M. Twenge, *iGen: Why Today's Super-Connected Kids Are Growing Up Less Rebellious, More Tolerant, Less Happy—and Completely Unprepared for Adulthood*. New York: Atria, 2017.

Internet Sources

Madelyn S. Gould and Alison M. Lake, "The Contagion of Suicidal Behavior," National Center for Biotechnology Information, 2013. www.ncbi.nlm.nih.gov/books/NBK207262.

Mayo Clinic Staff, "Suicide and Suicidal Thoughts," Mayo Clinic, August 28, 2015. www.mayoclinic.org/diseases-conditions/suicide/basics/risk-factors/con-20033954.

Robert T. Muller, "Antidepressants and Teen Suicide," *Talking About Trauma* (blog), *Psychology Today*, May 31, 2013. www.psychologyto day.com/blog/talking-about-trauma/201305/antidepressants-and-teen-suicide.

National Institute of Mental Health, "Antidepressant Medications for Children and Adolescents: Information for Parents and Caregivers," National Institutes of Health. www.nimh.nih.gov/health/topics/child-and-adolescent-mental-health/antidepressant-medications-for-children-and-adolescents-information-for-parents-and-caregivers.shtml.

Peter Stanford, "Are Smartphones Making Our Children Mentally Ill?," *Telegraph* (London), March 21, 2015. www.telegraph.co.uk/news/health/children/11486167/Are-smartphones-making-our-children-mentally-ill.html.

Sabrina Tavernise, "Young Adolescents as Likely to Die from Suicide as from Traffic Accidents," *New York Times*, November 3, 2016. www.nytimes.com/2016/11/04/health/suicide-adolescents-traffic-deaths.html?mcubz=3.

Jean M. Twenge, "Have Smartphones Destroyed a Generation?," *Atlantic*, September 2017. www.theatlantic.com/magazine/archive/2017/09/has-the-smartphone-destroyed-a-generation/534198.

Index

About the Author

Bradley Steffens is a poet, novelist, and award-winning author of more than forty nonfiction books for children and young adults. He is a two-time recipient of the San Diego Book Award for Best Young Adult and Children's Nonfiction: His *Giants* won the 2005 award, and his *J.K. Rowling* claimed the 2007 prize. Steffens also received the Theodor S. Geisel Award for best book by a San Diego County author in 2007.